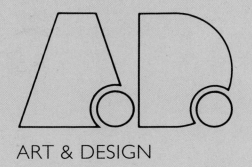

ART & DESIGN

EDITORIAL OFFICES:
42 LEINSTER GARDENS, LONDON W2 3AN
TEL: 071-402 2141 FAX: 071-723 9540

EDITOR
Dr Andreas C Papadakis

EDITORIAL TEAM: Nicola Hodges, Vivian
Constantinopoulos
DESIGN TEAM: Andrea Bettella (Senior
Designer), Annamarie Uhr, Jan Richter
BUSINESS MANAGER: Sheila de Vallée

SUBSCRIPTION OFFICES:
UK: VCH PUBLISHERS (UK) LTD
8 WELLINGTON COURT, WELLINGTON STREET
CAMBRIDGE CB1 1HZ UK

USA: VCH PUBLISHERS INC
SUITE 909, 220 EAST 23RD STREET
NEW YORK, NY 10010 USA

ALL OTHER COUNTRIES: VCH VERLAGS-
GESELLSCHAFT MBH
BOSCHSTRASSE 12, POSTFACH 101161
6940 WEINHEIM GERMANY

CONTENTS

William Stok, Apollo and
Daphne, *1979, montage*

*Zoe Zenghelis (with Elia
Zenghelis),* Hotel Sphinx, *1975,
oil on canvas*

Patrick Caulfield, Artist's
Studio, *detail, 1964, oil on
canvas*

BACK ISSUES

ART & DESIGN

1990 ANNUAL SUBSCRIPTION RATE (for six double issues inc p&p) *Art & Design*, UK/Eire only £45.00. USA $85. Rest of the World DM144. Reduced Student Rate: UK/Eire only £39.50. USA $75. Rest of the World DM128. Subscriptions may be backdated to any issue.

... 3 ABSTRACT ART
0 85670 919 0 £7.95

... 4 THE POST-AVANT-GARDE
0 85670 922 0 £7.95

... 5 BRITISH AND AMERICAN ART
0 85670 930 1 £7.95

... 6 SCULPTURE TODAY
0 85670 931 X £7.95

... 7 DAVID HOCKNEY
0 85670 935 2 £7.95

... 8 THE NEW MODERNISM
0 85670 940 9 £7.95

... 9 THE CLASSICAL SENSIBILITY
0 85670 948 4 £7.95

... 10 ART IN THE AGE OF PLURALISM
0 85670 957 3 £7.95

... 11 BRITISH ART NOW
0 85670 958 1 £7.95

... 12 THE NEW ROMANTICS
0 85670 956 5 £7.95

... 13 ITALIAN ART NOW
0 85670 993 X £7.95

... 14 40 UNDER 40
0 85670 995 6 £7.95

... 15 MALEVICH
0 85670 998 0 £7.95

... 16 NEW YORK NEW ART
1 85490 004 8 £7.95

... 17 GERMAN ART NOW
1 85490 023 4 £7.95

... 18 ASPECTS OF MODERN ART
1 85490 020 X £7.95

... 19 NEW ART INTERNATIONAL
1 85490 018 8 £7.95

... 20 ART & THE TECTONIC
1 85490 037 4 £7.95

... 21 ART MEETS SCIENCE & SPIRITUALITY
1 85490 038 2 £7.95

... 22 NEW MUSEOLOGY
0 32107 141 8 £7.95

... 23 THE RURALISTS
1 85490 123 0 £7.95

... 24 POP ART
1 85490 134 6 £7.95

... 25 MARKING THE CITY BOUNDARIES
1 85490 135 4 £9.95

... 26 CONTEMPORARY PAINTINGS
1 85490 154 0 £9.95

ARCHITECTURAL DESIGN

1990 ANNUAL SUBSCRIPTION RATE (for six double issues inc p&p) *Architectural Design*, UK/Eire only £55.00. USA $99.50. Rest of World DM178. Reduced Student Rate: UK/Eire only £45. USA $89.50. Rest of World DM144. Subscriptions may be backdated to any issue.

... 1 ARATA ISOZAKI
0 85670 330 3 £3.95

... 3 TAFURI/CULOT/KRIER
0 85670 355 9 £3.95

... 11 SURREALISM
0 85670 409 1 £6.95

... 14 HAND-BUILT HORNBY
0 85670 430 X £3.95

... 16 BRUCE GOFF
0 85670 432 6 £6.95

... 19 SAINSBURY CENTRE
0 85670 563 2 £3.95

... 20 ROMA INTERROTTA
0 85670 560 8 £6.95

... 21 LEON BATTISTA ALBERTI
0 85670 559 4 £6.95

... 22 HAWKSMOOR'S CHRISTCHURCH
0 85670 650 7 £3.95

... 23 NEO-CLASSICISM
0 85670 626 4 £6.95

... 24 BRITAIN IN THE THIRTIES
0 85670 627 2 £6.95

... 25 AALTO AND AFTER
0 85670 701 5 £4.95

... 27 VIOLLET-LE-DUC
0 85670 688 4 £6.95

... 31 URBANITY
0 85670 746 5 £6.95

... 33 BRITISH ARCHITECTS 1981
0 85670 750 3 £6.95

... 34 ROMANTIC HOUSES
0 85670 754 6 £4.95

... 37 ANGLO AMERICAN SUBURB
0 85670 690 6 £6.95

... 38 CURRENT PROJECTS
0 85670 768 6 £4.95

... 44 FOREST EDGE & POST-WAR BERLIN
0 85670 789 9 £8.95

... 46 DOLLS' HOUSES
0 85670 827 5 £8.95

... 47 THE RUSSIAN AVANT-GARDE
0 85670 832 1 £8.95

... 49 ELEMENTS OF ARCHITECTURE
0 85670 834 8 £8.95

... 51 URBANISM
0 85670 843 7 £8.95

... 52 BRITISH ARCHITECTURE 1984
0 85670 845 3 £8.95

... 53 BUILDING & RATIONAL ARCH
0 85670 848 8 £8.95

... 54 LEON KRIER
0 85670 844 5 £8.95

... 55 IAKOV CHERNIKHOV
0 85670 841 0 £8.95

... 56 UIA CAIRO INT. EXHIB.
0 85670 852 6 £8.95

... 57 AMERICAN ARCHITECTURE
0 85670 855 0 £8.95

... 58 REVISION OF THE MODERN
0 85670 861 5 £8.95

... 59 SCHOOL OF VENICE
0 85670 853 4 £8.95

... 60 LE CORBUSIER ARCHIVE
0 85670 696 5 £8.95

... 61 DESIGNING A HOUSE
0 85670 888 7 £8.95

... 62 VIENNA DREAM AND REALITY
0 85670 886 0 £8.95

... 63 NATIONAL GALLERY
0 85670 884 4 £8.95

... 7/86 TRADITION, INVENTION & CONVENTION, EUROPEAN CITY BUILDING
0 85670 903 4 £3.95

... 9/86 AMERICAN URBANISM 1
0 85670 905 0 £3.95

... 64 A HOUSE FOR TODAY
0 85670 911 5 £8.95

... 12/86 TADAO ANDO, TAKEFUMA AIDA, BASIL BAYATI
0 85670 906 9 £3.95

... 66 NEOCLASSICAL ARCHITECTURE IN COPENHAGEN & ATHENS
0 85670 887 9 £8.95

... 67 TRADITION & ARCHITECTURE
0 85670 890 9 £8.95

... 68 SOVIET ARCHITECTURE
0 85670 920 4 £8.95

... 69 ARCHITECTURE OF DEMOCRACY
0 85670 923 9 £8.95

... 70 ENGINEERING & ARCHITECTURE
0 85670 932 8 £8.95

... 71 THE NEW CLASSICISM
0 85670 938 7 £8.95

... 72 DECONSTRUCTION IN ARCHITECTURE
0 85670 941 7 £8.95

... 73 JAPANESE ARCHITECTURE
0 85670 950 6 £8.95

... 74 CONTEMPORARY ARCH
0 85670 953 0 £8.95

... 75 IMITATION & INNOVATION
0 85670 954 9 £8.95

... 76 NEW DIRECTIONS IN CURRENT ARCHITECTURE
0 85670 992 1 £8.95

... 77 DECONSTRUCTION II
0 85670 994 8 £8.95

... 78 DRAWING INTO ARCHITECTURE
0 85670 997 2 £8.95

... 79 PRINCE CHARLES & ARCH. DEBATE
1 85490 021 8 £8.95

... 80 RUSSIAN CONSTRUCTIVISM & CHERNIKHOV
1 85490 019 6 £8.95

... 81 RECONSTRUCTION/DECONSTRUCTION
1 85490 000 5 £8.95

... 82 WEXNER CENTER FOR THE VISUAL ARTS
1 85490 027 7 £8.95

... 83 URBAN CONCEPTS
0 85670 955 7 £8.95

... 84 NEW ARCHITECTURE
1 85490 029 3 £8.95

... 85 STIRLING, WILFORD & ASSOCIATES
1 85490 042 0 £8.95

... 86 THE NEW MODERN AESTHETIC
1 85490 043 9 £8.95

... 87 DECONSTRUCTION III
1 85490 050 1 £8.95

... 88 POST-MODERNISM ON TRIAL
1 85490 044 7 £8.95

... 89 A NEW SPIRIT IN ARCHITECTURE
1 85490 092 7 £8.95

... 90 ASPECTS OF MODERN ARCHITECTURE
1 85490 102 8 £8.95

... 91 POST-MODERN TRIUMPHS IN LONDON
1 85490 103 6 £8.95

... 92 BERLIN TOMORROW
1 85490 104 4 £8.95

... 93 THE AVANT-GARDE: RUSSIAN ARCH
1 85490 077 3 £8.95

... 94 NEW MUSEUMS
1 85490 117 6 £8.95

... 95 MODERN PLURALISM – Just exactly what is going on?
1 85490 124 9 £9.95

... 96 FREE SPACE ARCHITECTURE
1 85490 127 3 £9.95

... 97 PATERNOSTER SQUARE
1 85490 131 1 £9.95

... 98 POP ARCHITECTURE
1 85490 133 8 £9.95

... 99 JAPANESE ARCHITECTURE II
1 85490 132 1 £9.95

... 100 THEORY AND EXPERIMENTATION
1 85490 138 9 £9.95

ARCHITECTURAL MONOGRAPHS

SUBSCRIPTION RATES (for six issues inc p&p, publication irregular) *Architectural Monographs*, UK/Eire only £80.00. USA $150. Rest of World DM 255. Reduced Student Rate: UK/Eire only £75. USA $140. Rest of World DM239. Subscriptions may be backdated to any issue.

... 4 ALVAR AALTO
0 85670 421 0 £12.95

... 6 EDWIN LUTYENS Rev. Edn
0 85670 422 9 £12.95

... 8 JOHN SOANE
0 85670 830 5 HB£17.50
0 85670 805 4 PB £12.95

... 9 TERRY FARRELL
0 85670 851 8 HB£17.50
0 85670 842 9 PB£12.95

... 10 RICHARD ROGERS
0 85670 862 3 HB£17.50
0 85670 786 4 PB£12.95

... 11 MIES VAN DER ROHE
0 85670 685 X PB£12.95

... 12 LE CORBUSIER: Early Work
0 85670 892 5 HB£17.50
0 85670 804 6 PB£12.95

... 13 HASSAN FATHY
0 85670 921 2 HB£17.50
0 85670 918 2 PB£12.95

... 14 TADAO ANDO
1 85490 010 2 HB£17.50
1 85490 007 2 PB£12.95

... AHRENDS, BURTON & KORALEK
0 85670 929 8 HB £19.95
0 85670 927 1 PB £14.95

... DANIEL LIBESKIND
1 85490 094 3 HB £19.95
1 85490 097 8 PB £14.95

... ROBERT STERN
1 85490 011 0 HB £19.95
1 85490 008 0 PB £14.95

... FOSTER ASSOCIATES
1 85490 108 7 HB £19.95
1 85490 111 7 PB £14.95

... VENTURI SCOTT BROWN
1 85490 093 5 HB £19.95
1 85490 098 6 PB £14.95

... FRANK LLOYD WRIGHT
1 85490 105 2 HB £19.95
1 85490 110 9 PB £14.95

... C.F.A. VOYSEY
1 85490 031 5 HB£17.50
1 85490 032 3 PB£12.95

UIA JOURNAL

Published in cooperation with the International Union of Architects. SUBSCRIPTION RATES (for four issues inc p&p, publication irregular) *UIA Journal*, UK/Eire only £55. USA $99.50. Rest of World DM175. Reduced Student Rate: UK/Eire only £49.50. USA $89.50. Rest of World DM158.

... 1 VISION OF THE MODERN
RP/ND 0 85670 915 8 PB £12.95

... 2 DECONSTRUCTION – A STUDENT GUIDE
1 85490 035 8 PB £12.95

JOURNAL OF PHILOSOPHY AND THE VISUAL ARTS

SUBSCRIPTION RATES (for four issues inc p&p, publication irregular) *Journal of Philosophy and the Visual Arts*, UK/Eire only £49.50. USA $100. Rest of World DM160. Reduced Student Rate: UK/Eire only £45. USA $90. Rest of World DM144.

... PHILOSOPHY & THE VISUAL ARTS
0 85670 966 2 PB £12.95

... PHILOSOPHY & ARCHITECTURE
1 85490 016 1 PB £12.95

... ARCHITECTURE-SPACE-PAINTING
1 85490 136 2 PB £12.95

ART & DESIGN

Going beyond the transience of much contemporary art criticism, *Art & Design* offers an in-depth exploration of the underlying patterns of contemporary art. The magazine draws its themes from new exhibitions, symposia and critical definitions and establishes a forum through which to confront the accelerating history of an art world dominated by the quest for the new. Leading international artists, critics, philosophers, curators and collectors contributing to the debate include Robert Rosenblum, Demosthenes Davvetas, Donald Kuspit, Walter Grasskamp, Thomas Lawson, Jeff Koons, Victor Burgin, Jean-François Lyotard, Daniel Buren and Joseph Kosuth. Critical essays are combined with interviews and artists' statements in an attempt to create a dialogue between art and criticism, frequently highlighting the tension existing between critical philosophical interpretations and the intentions of the artists themselves.

Each issue is founded on a new theme, exploring the art of individual centres such as Berlin, London and New York, examining the work of artists experimenting in particular media, or expanding on definitions and issues such as the use of photography and new computer technology, the appropriation of the mass media or the interaction between art and architecture – particularly in new museum design. The magazine also casts a critical glance back to the early decades of the 20th century in an attempt to redefine the past and establish the significance and credibility of new art in the context of historical movements.

Recent issues have included, *German Art Now, Aspects of Modern Art, New Art International, Art & the Tectonic, Art meets Science and Spirituality, New Museology, The Ruralists, Pop Art, Marking the City Boundaries and Contemporary Painting.*

Subscribe Now!

VI

transporting them inside. The sheet, like the glass pane of the mirror, is used to divide the present – the director Fellini making the film (the cone of vision of the beholder) from the past – the mirroring in his memory of himself as a child on the other side of the sheet in the scene the director is describing to us.

In *The Forest of Architecture*, the bust of Andreas Papadakis looks towards the forest and does not make up part of the sculptural

The Gargoyle, *1978*

group in so far as he is not an architect and it is clear that his position on the right, at the edge of the painting, symmetrically balancing the curtain on the left, acquires the same function: putting the picture into focus. When the painting was commissioned and it was suggested that I should portray myself, I first thought of using my shadow projected on the curtain. Usually,

The Forest of Architecture, *1990*

V

WILLIAM STOK
THE FOREST OF ARCHITECTURE

Commissioned by Andreas Papadakis, *The Forest of Architecture* represents a forest, suggesting a theatrical background with a drawn back curtain on the left focusing attention on the seven portrait busts (seven being the symbolic number of the gods) of Demetri Porphyrios, Charles Jencks, Peter Eisenman, Leon Krier, Robert Graves, James Stirling and Andreas Papadakis; the figures most directly involved in *Architectural Design* magazine. This sculptural group presented in a public place is unveiled at its inauguration ceremony as if freed from the curtain which surrounded it. In deciding how best to represent the architects I could simply have chosen to paint them in a naturalistic manner, possibly holding the building which best represents each of them to enhance a more detailed, literal aspect of their individuality. However, influenced by my exhibition *Apollo and Daphne* (1988), where I traced the metamorphosis of Daphne into a tree paralleling the historical transformation of the primitive architectural structure of trees into columns (*qv* Vitruvius), in a symbolic, not naturalistic manner, my interest was directed towards a more general vision. Presenting the architects as sculptures in a forest gave emphasis to the basic elements of building construction: stone (the busts) and wood (the trees).

There is very little difference in primitive man's relationship to stone and to the tree; in fact both were worshipped as the place of the gods or as a god in their own right. This was probably due to the qualities inherent in each material – even today stone and oak are regarded as symbols of durability – but also because of primitive man's need to project his human shape in a god. Finding the right shape in both stone and tree, made them ideal to be sculpted into an approximation of the human figure. Stones were used to mark the boundaries of a place of worship as well as land dividers, whilst a single enormous tree was developed in mythology grown from a flat earth to hold a curved sky (the Finns later replacing it with a central column). The tree is one of the recurrent themes of my work because of its near human stillness. Its ambiguity between 'life' and 'rigidity' place the tree between man and sculpture: so I have used it as a metaphor for 'people' in the sculptures from 1969-75, substituted it sometimes by the column, from 1981, or due to its property of regeneration, used it to symbolise life or metamorphosis in the photographs and paintings, from 1979-90.

In 1972 I began to include perspective in my visual vocabulary unifying the sculptures of trees by using long converging platforms, to give an illusory perspective to the enormous scenic frames facing the beholder, to bring the sculpture into focus. The frame, although it is three dimensional (thus allowing it to be seen from any angle) always conceived as constricting the spectator to look at the work from one sole viewpoint, in fact conditioning the beholder to stand on a single spot or go along a pre-arranged route. When years later in the environment *The Gargoyle* (1978), the sculpture was seen through a gate put in front of the doorway of the gallery or in *Past, Present, Future* (1977) five dancing figures on transparent plastic were drawn decreasing in size as their position in the room was further away from the onlooker; I was developing the frame with the same function as used in the tree sculpture into the architectural structure itself.

An image which I have always found helpful in portraying this concept literally is the curtain. When Fellini in the film *8 1/2* uses a sheet hanging on a washing line, it has the clear role of a filter between the past: Fellini as a child – playing on the far side of the sheet; and the present – the courtyard – on this side of the sheet, which opens up to the spectators, like a theatrical stage,

Oedipus Rex, *1976*

tive way in which I have painted the trees allowed the possibility of adding others in an infinite procession without any great change – as if they were modulars. If the image had been painted in great detail it wouldn't have helped the impact of the whole image. On the other hand, a shape of great size and elongated, as in this painting, generates the need to walk past the canvas to be able to experience and incidentally repeat the same horizontal ambulatory motion which occurred when it was painted. The mythological environment which I have used is not a landscape, but rather one of the types of classical scene to which any connoisseur of art is already accustomed, added to the fact that the eye runs over the trees without noting any significant stresses, rendering the reading more fluid, focusing the attention more clearly on the portraits.

What has influenced the choice of huge horizontal painting is film, the editing of an image framed by the use of the camera and the elongated shape bringing to mind cinemascope. I am very myopic so I need to be physically very close to the Big Screen and so almost engulfed by it, with the sensation of finding myself inside the 'whale's stomach', likewise a cinema-goer drawn into the film plot becomes one of the actors.

I have often discovered metaphysical vibrations in frescoes, particularly in Pompeii, or in those by Piero della Francesca, Giotto, Masaccio, Simone Martini. Because they are presented like a thin veil in suspension imperceptibly absorbed into the will, they never give the impression of the materiality of the colour; the white lime gives a sense of rarefication, accentuated by the deterioration of time. My interest is not in how these works were originally printed (Renaissance artists drew inspiration from Greek sculptures being unaware that they were originally coloured), nor in the effect of flatness and discoloration, due to the passage of time, as an end in itself (unlike Panofsky's 'love of mould') but in the significance that I have gained from them: a stimulus to memory and imagination. For this reason I prefer to use a limited range of colour, becoming less descriptive, leaving the door open to our sensations, letting us draw closer with less, to reality. Many film directors have returned to the use of black and white because it is less tangible, less real, can enter into another dimension. Often in these frescoes all that remains is the basic colour which was originally dominant in a certain figure, without the colours that constitute the half-tones, rendering the image flat, like a drawing which has been superimposed by a single tint, giving the main focus to the outline.

Exactly this is predominant in the environment *Past, Present, Future* where the line contains the flat colour inside dancing figures which are suspended to the centre of sheets of plastic fixed to the ceiling as if enormous figures have passed through leaving a trace of their passage, perhaps reminiscent of the naked figures of Yves Klein, which, covered in pigment, leave a trace of their bodies on the virgin canvas. I am fascinated by the image in the fall of Sodom and Gomorrah of Lot's wife who turns round and is transformed into salt; the figures in Pompeii, solidified in the lava of Vesuvius which has preserved their final act. In *The Forest of Architecture*, for the first time I portray people who signify nothing other than themselves; they are not actors, nor disguised in other clothing, yet they are not completely real as they have been transformed into stone. The 'frozen act' of sculpture, like the limitation of the black and white medium in film or the rarefication of old frescoes, is some kind of mask, a device to elude, and able to come closer to the truth.

Mural for Charles Jencks' Thematic House, *1984*

when I need to be included in a painting, I portray my brother, who I have always felt to be my 'alter ego', using him to act my part as a film director might do. In this case, noticing in the painting the position of Andreas Papadakis who is indicating the scene and who has acted as a frame to the contemporary architectural scene, he was clearly the candidate to become the cine-camera which I looked through.

In this project, the huge, thin, horizontal

Past, Present, Future, 1978

shape is stretched between what might be called two 'pillars', the curtain on the left hand side and the bust of the patron on the right side, bringing to mind a scroll. In trying to turn the 'scroll', the passage of time changes the names of the architects portrayed, presenting the future, or in a reverse direction, the past architectural scene. The casual manner and the repeti-

BOOKS

BOOKS RECEIVED:

DIZIONARIO DEL FARE ARTE CONTEMPORANEO *by Lara Vinca Masini, Universale Sansoni, Firenze, 1992, 422pp, b/w ills, PB L50,000*

NARRATIVE, INNOVATION, INCO-HERANCE *by Michael Boardman, Duke University Press, Durham, North Carolina, 1992, 227pp, HB price N/A*

GRAPHIC DESIGN MADE DIFFI-CULT *by Bob Gill, Chapman and Hall, London, 1992, 160pp, colour ills, HB £22.00*

ON INNOVATIVE ART(IST)S: Rec-ollections of an Expanding Field *by Richard Kostelanetz, McFarland and Co, Folkestone,1992, 356pp, HB £28.50*

NAKED AUTHORITY: The Body in Western Painting 1830-1908 *by Marcia Pointon, Cambridge University Press, Cambridge, 1990, 160pp, b/w ills, PB £14.95*

FRENCH ARCHITECTURE AND ORNAMENT DRAWINGS OF THE EIGHTEENTH CENTURY *by Mary L Myers, The Metropolitan Museum of Art, New York, 1992, 256pp, colour ills, HB price N/A*

PHILOSOPHICAL AESTHETICS *by Oswald Hanfling, Blackwell, Oxford, 1992, 485pp, colour ills, HB £35.00 PB £10.95*

THE GOTHIC CATHEDRAL *by Christopher Wilson, Thames & Hudson, London, 1992, 304pp, b/w ills, PB £12.95*

THE MEANING OF GARDENS *edited by Mark Francis and Randolph T Hester Jr, MIT Press, Cambridge, 1992, 280pp, b/w ills, PB £20.50*

SEVEN YEARS WITH THE GROUP OF SEVEN *by Joyce Putman, The Quarry Press, Kingston, Ontario, 1992, 140pp, colour ills, HB price N/A*

RAILWAY POSTERS 1923-1947 *by Beverly Cole and Richard Durack, Laurence King, London, 1992, 160pp, colour ills, PB £14.95*

WILLIAM MORRIS: Design and Enterprise in Victorian Britain *by*

LITTLE PIG by Akumal Ramachander and illustrated by Stasys Eidrigevicius, Viking, London, 1992, 29pp, colour ills, HB £9.99
'A disturbing and haunting morality tale; a potent argument for vegetarianism; a metaphor for the holocaust; a classic tale of trust and betrayal or just a simple children's story', Ramachander's poignant tale is open to many different interpretations. *Little Pig* is a powerful story dealing with cruelty and betrayal by the strong over the weak, written in a clear and succinct style with a memorable set of illustrations by Lithuanian artist Stasys Eidrigevicius.

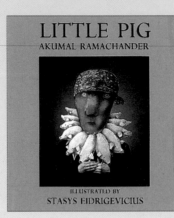

BERLIN! BERLIN! Its Culture, Its Times by Michael Farr, Kyle Cathie Ltd, London, 1992, 216pp, b/w ills, HB £18.99
A city which has fascinated architects, artists and historians alike, Berlin has once again come into the limelight, rising out of the ashes of Communism, tempting authors in particular to research its sometimes illustrious, sometimes threatening past. Michael Farr, appointed chief correspondent in Germany for *The Daily Telegraph* between 1981 and 1987, has traced the foundation of Berlin from its medieval beginnings to the present day, recording tales of famous Berliners and reflecting on the political roller-coaster which Berlin has undergone in its history.

NUDES IN BUDAPEST by James Cotier, AKTOK, London, 1992, b/w ills, HB price N/A
Cortier's collection of black and white photographs allow us a sympathetic insight into the ageing process and the deterioration of

youth and flesh that we all have to accept as the inevitable. Cortier chose his subjects and took the photographs in Budapest at a Turkish bath where the decaying Art Deco architecture gently reflects the natural state of his sitters: unabashed Eastern European people who, having survived a lifetime of hardship and political oppression where youth and beauty was almost inconsequential, feel relaxed and at ease with their wrinkled, sometimes sagging bodies. Throughout this book Cortier gives old people a dignity which is not often acknowledged. As we turn the pages and cast our eye over the softly lit sitters, it dawns upon us that old age need not be a fearful expectation: a certain kind of wisdom and beauty comes with it.

LASTING LETTERS: An Inscription for the Abbots of St Albans edited by Rosamond McKitteriot and Lida Lopes Cardozo, Cardozo Kindersley Editions, Cambridge, 1992, 96pp, b/w ills, HB £25.00 and PB £14.95
This book was inspired by a slab of Welsh slate in the Abbey of St Albans which commemorates the abbots who died between 1077 and 1401 and whose remains have recently been buried beneath the slate after an extensive excavation project. The slate was designed and cut by David Kindersley and together with the book is a celebration of the achievements of the abbots and the period of book production when meticulous detail and the greatest of patience embodied the feeling of an age.

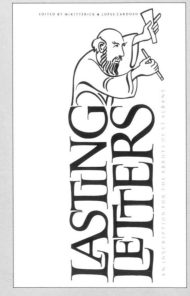

ORNAMENTAL DESIGNS FROM ARCHITECTURAL SHEET METAL: The Complete Broschart And Braun Catalogue c 1900 preface by Roger W Moss, The Athenaeum of Philadelphia and Dover Publications Inc, New York, 78pp, b/w ills, PB £8.95
An unabridged and unaltered reproduction of the original *Artistic Sheet Metal Ornaments* published c 1900, this illustrated book depicts over 1,000 sheet metal designs by a major American supplier. Today the book will be important to both architectural historians and home enthusiasts, being an invaluable reference to the ornamental features which enriched and were an essential feature of Victorian homes and buildings.

THE BRITISH COUNCIL, MANCHESTER: Catalogue of Works of Art Manchester, 1992, 55pp, colour ills, PB price N/A
In the last few years the British Council has opened cultural centres throughout the world to exhibit and celebrate British art, craft and design. Recently, the Council's cultural headquarters moved from London to Manchester, providing the exceptional opportunity to display British art created overseas. Along with this the Council commissioned a monumental timepiece by the sculptor Bill Woodrow and an atrium carpet by Patrick Caulfield, both of which have been integrated into the daily workings of the office space rather than being mere museum exhibits. Further works on display shown in this catalogue include post-war embroidery, ceramics commemorating the Gulf War and an installation of a Penzance fish shop.

THE BAUHAUS: A Japanese Perspective and a Profile of Hans and Florence Schust Knoll by Akio Izutsu, translated by Brian Harrison, Kajima Institute Publishing Co Ltd, 1992, 203pp, colour ills, HB price N/A
The Bauhaus is a subject which has had much written about it and in this book it is approached from a refreshingly new angle, focusing on the Japanese perspective of the renowned art school. Written in both Japanese and English, the

Charles Harvey and Jon Press, Manchester University Press, Manchester, 1992, 257pp, b/w ills, PB £12.95

DENNIS OPPENHEIM: Selected Works 1967-1990 by Alanna Heiss with an essay by Thomas McEvilley, Abrams, New York, 1992, 200pp, colour ills, HB £30.00

MARK TANSEY : Visions and Revisions by Arthur C Danto, Abrams, New York, 1992, 142pp, colour ills, HB £25.00

ART: THE WAY IT IS (fourth edition) by John Adkins Richardson, Abrams, New York, 1992, 416 pp, colour ills, HB £ 35.00

LYLE PRICE GUIDE TO ART NOUVEAU AND DECO by Tony Curtis, Lyle Publications, Hove, 1992, 447pp, colour ills, £14.95

EVALUATING AND PREDICTING DESIGN PERFORMANCE edited by Yehuda E Kalay, John Wiley & Sons, New York, 1992, 404pp, b/w ills, HB price N/A

THEO VAN DOESBURG: PAINTER AND ARCHITECT by Evert van Straten, SDU Publications, The Hague, 1988, 265pp, colour ills, HB price N/A

INSIDE OUT: Design Procedures for Passive Environmental Technologies (Second Edition), John Wiley & Sons, New York, 1992, 332pp, b/w ills, PB price N/A

JOSEPH BEUYS: DIE MULTIPLES by Jörg Schellmann Schirmer, Mosel Verlag, Munich,1992, 588pp, b/w ills, HB price N/A

WORLD DESIGN: Nationalism and Globalism in Design by Hugh Aldersey-Williams, Rizzoli, New York, 1992, 204pp, colour ills, HB £29.95

DESIGN DRAWING TECHNIQUES FOR ARCHITECTS, GRAPHIC DESIGNERS AND ARTISTS by Tom Porter and Sue Goodman, Butterworth Heinemann, Oxford, 1992, 357pp, b/w ills, PB 14.95

DECORATING MAGIC by John Sutcliffe, Frances Lincoln, London, 1992, 192pp, colour ills, HB £18.95

Graham Arnold, The Room, *1991, oil on board, 91.4x122 cm, from* Graham Arnold: A Retrospective *by Ol Syllu, The Machynlleth Tabernacle Trustees, Powys, 1992, 61pp, colour ills, PB price N/A*

book investigates the foundation of the Bauhaus, the influence it had upon Japanese art and upon the furniture designs of Hans and Florence Schust Knoll. This is a highly informative book, especially for those interested in the wider implications the Bauhaus had for the art world.

PROJECTIVE ORNAMENT by Claude Bragdon, Dover Publications Inc, New York, 1992, 79pp, b/w ills, PB £3.95
Claude Bragdon, the famous American architect and art theorist invites us in this book to enter into the realm of the geometry of the fourth dimension as a source for design ideas making it possible for

us to investigate the field which he believes is the foundation of formal beauty.

CONTEMPORARY AMERICAN LANDSCAPE PHOTOGRAPHY, University of New Mexico Press, 1992, 176pp, b/w and colour ills, HB $50.00, PB $35.00
This catalogue to a major exhibit of landscape photography presented by the Smithsonian Institution's National Museum of American Art includes three essays ranging from a review of landscape photography by Merry A Foresta to reflections on the social meaning of landscape by Karal Ann Marling and on geological time by naturalist Steven Jay Gould. It is entitled 'Between Home and Heaven' because 'today photographers chart a territory between the necessity of society making its home on Earth and the hope that such a home can be a heaven on earth'.

PURPLE, WHITE AND GREEN by Diane Atkinson, Pentagram Design Ltd, London, 1992, colour ills, price N/A

Focusing upon the colours adopted by the Suffragette Movement, *Purple, White and Green* gives a short history of the campaign explaining the rationale behind the chosen colours. As an accompaniment to the text, there are illustrations of mementos from the exhibition at the Museum of London giving examples of the way in which the Suffragettes ruthlessly used their colours in mass merchandising and marketing, with objects ranging from Christmas cards to jewellery.

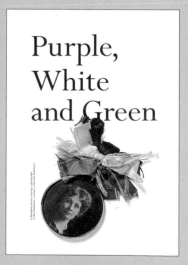

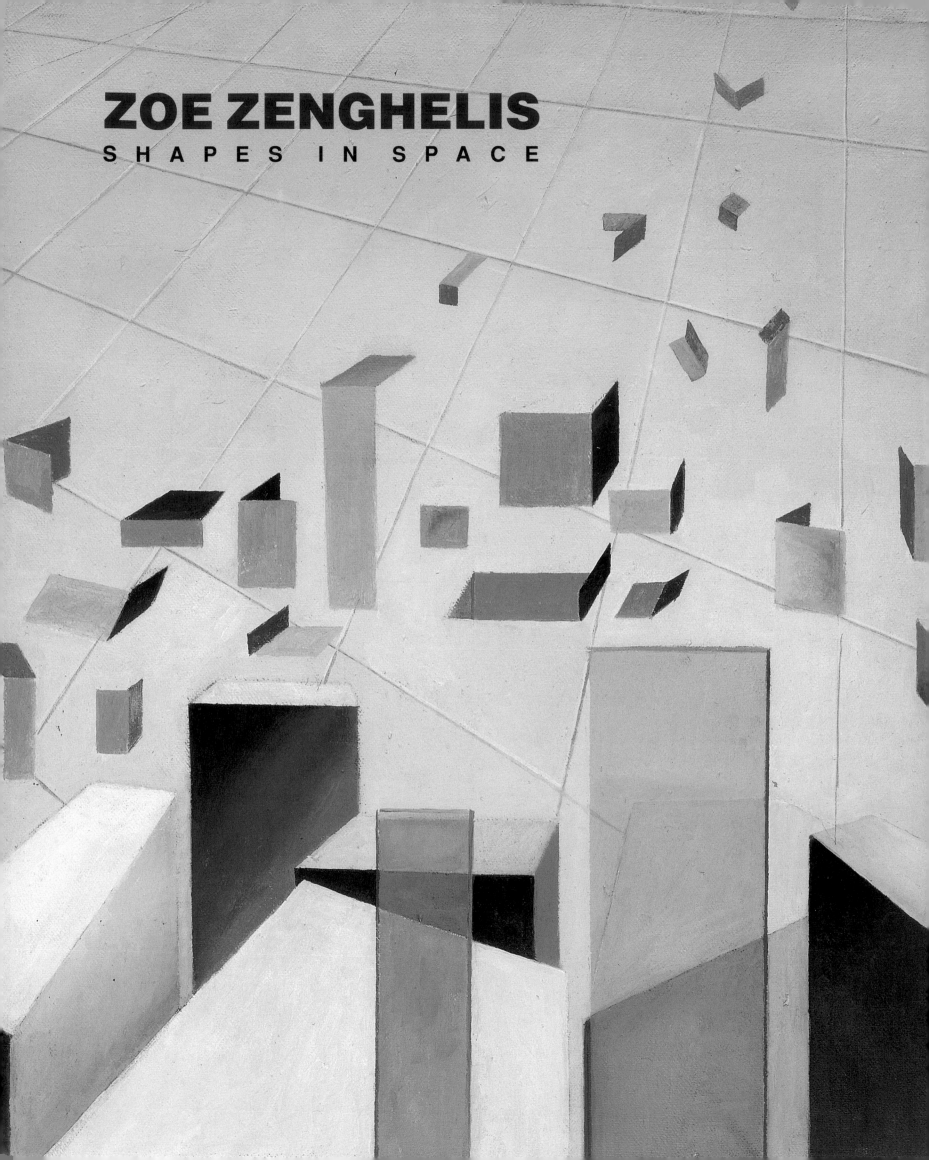

ZOE ZENGHELIS
SHAPES IN SPACE

Marina **Vaizey**

Zoe Zenghelis trained as a theatrical designer and painter and worked for a substantial period as a founder member of OMA (Office for Metropolitan Architecture), realising for presentation professional and conjectural schemes. She is a specialist in colour, a professional who teaches the subject, formalised as a Colour Workshop at the Architectural Association. Colour is a concern of crucial importance to architects and designers – yet, paradoxically, her captivating paintings are orchestrations dominated by silvery cool blues and greys. Occasionally, there is a complementary pinky-orange, sometimes even a sharp yellow. But the basic tonality is cool: and these refreshing and deliberately restricted tones and hues describe and delineate her subject matter, extracted, quarried and imagined from a long involvement with art – and architecture. A huge range of colour is suggested almost by its absence, just as black and white photography can at times resonate with far greater subtlety than colour.

Her paintings and watercolours exist brilliantly in the present by looking both to the past and the future. They cannot be read without a sense of the mediterranean, and the architecture of classic civilisation; a sense of the coastline is often present, in the suggestion of a horizon, a limitless sky. Yet the imagery is quintessentially modern and modernist: it is an imagery of the fragment, the collage, the assemblage, the parts standing for the whole, and often greater than the whole. Such suggestiveness, such coding, is a modernist idiom.

Zenghelis begins with of course a concept, goes on to the conjectural, and enters the realm of the imagination. Her use of the architectural, the placing of objects in space, is curiously unconfined. There are surprisingly few artists dealing with the ideas and ideals of architecture even in the twentieth century, a century which it will be seen is obsessed with architecture, and the ways in which buildings embody notions of the past to invigorate the present. Utopian ideals were conjured up in the profoundly idealistic and tragically flawed attempts at public planning, where unusually such planning was to go forward at times not for the glorification of the state but the comfort of its people.

The sheer startling scale of industrial architecture, and the extraordinary growth of the skyscraper, have inspired strikingly little visual response on the part of artists. There is no Piranesi of our times. Artists have been fascinated with enclosed space: the interior has been an absorbing subject. Even the architecture of the metaphysical artists and surrealists – de Chirico, for example – has been based on the contained Italian town, its piazzas and squares, outdoor rooms. In contrast, artists such as Kandinsky, Miró and the American Al Held have played with conventional notions of perspective, and flung, with a choreography of abandon, fragments in space, (sometimes as in the case of Held, with quite terrifying density), anticipating the realisation of weightlessness in the pre-space age.

Curiously, in Britain, a number of women artists – Deanna Petherbridge, Tess Jaray, Margaret Priest – have explored the abstracted interior. Buildings as such have inspired, in very different ways, the art of Brendan Neiland, concerned with the facade, the glitter of glass and metal, and Ben Johnson, who, intellectual yet as fiercely immediate as Al Held, has played with perspective. Ben Johnson does use specific buildings as catalyst and inspiration; but in his mobile for ITN, and some of his latest paintings, he is utilising the architectural fragment or an isolated form, even a detail, in space.

These are painters. Yet, recently, artists have certainly, in three dimensional forms, referred – at times almost obsessionally – to architecture. Sculptors in particular, of course, from Sir Anthony Caro to Julian Opie, have conjured up an imaginary architecture. The enormous public work of Dani Karavan is an architecture without building. Much of the finest public art can only exist and take its meaning from an architectural context and setting, often an outdoor room: Richard Serra's Fulcrum at Broadgate is a brilliant use of enclosed outdoor space, a space for passing through, and a space which is simultaneously exit and entrance. The current obsession with installation is an obsession with inhabiting space, often space within space.

It is perhaps the nature of their work, their techniques and their way of thinking that means that those who work with three dimensional form have most readily shared in the architecture fervour that is currently characterising aesthetic debate. This has become a beguiling conceit in the work of Langland & Bell, who make sculptures, often wall hanging, which are like architectural models, both fantasised and radically simplified.

Architects themselves work from two dimensions into three. Zoe Zenghelis has spent her working life with architects, and has deliberately confined her artistic life to working on a flat surface. Architects, Zoe Zenghelis has said, don't think colour –

just black lines on white pages. She herself works straight onto the surface with colour, without lines. Space is controlled with colour; colour makes things bigger and smaller. Her paintings deploy, like characters in a plot, screens, totems, free standing columns, pillars, casting shadows in spaces lit all over. The light source is diffuse; shadows are used as shapes in themselves.

In Zenghelis' contained paintings, there is, again paradoxically, a suggestion of space stretching far beyond our perception, a celestial city, without limits. The eye is as absorbed by the space between the forms as the forms themselves, set into informal procession.

But it is picture making beyond the stage, set somewhere between the contrived and the natural, the abstract and the representational. These imaginary spaces are inspired as much by the urban grid of London, the cities of concrete, as the islands of the Ionian Sea, their white gleaming houses bleached by light, the surrounding water both absorbing and reflecting the glittering sky. Space and territory, our own and others, is a question of politics and aesthetics. These paintings hint at imagination's journey. As the poet EE Cummings once phrased it, it is always the beautiful answer who asks the beautiful question.

Poeticising the urban environment
An interview with Zoe Zenghelis

Painting represents only one aspect of your work, how do you conciliate all your activities ?

My work can be divided into three areas: my teaching at the Architectural Association, the work I have done for OMA (Office for Metropolitan Architecture) and my work as a painter in my own right.

What does your teaching consist of ?

I teach at the AA together with Madelon

Vriesendorp. We run the 'Colour Workshop' which belongs to the Communication Department together with photography, etching, video and life drawing. In our workshop we try to help the students express their projects in a visual way. Colour is basic to our perception of the world, though to most architectural students it comes at best as an afterthought. Structure and form are their main concerns. We try to show them that colour is an integral part of the design process, inspiring and helping to develop new ideas. The first essential of practical colour study is to develop the skill to obtain any colour quickly and accurately. Technically painting is about getting precisely the right amount of precisely the right colour in precisely the right places. With colour you can convey mood, enlarge or reduce scale, intensify sensation and provide stimulation or relaxation. You can make areas advance or retreat, blend or stand out so colour can control space and proportions in buildings. Often this power is being used to cover up inhumane conditions or bad design. Students must develop an honest approach to representation and the ability to master the painting of different materials (ie marble, metal, glass, stone etc), their textures or colour so as to conceive a building in its totality.

What exactly were you doing in the Office for Metropolitan Architecture ?

In 1972 Rem Koolhaas, Elia Zenghelis, Madelon Vriesendorp and myself (two architects and two painters) founded OMA. Madelon and I were doing the presentations of the architectural designs, for exhibitions, competitions and publications. The office survived the first years from the sale of these paintings. When 'real' work started coming in, we became less needed and started spending much more time on our own painting and teaching.

Why is architecture so present in your painting ?

In my paintings I use architectural signs to develop analogies between space, lines and shapes and between forms as in columns and the building and sculptures and the building. I use architectural shapes mainly because of my architectural background but otherwise I could just as well use, for instance, trees or human figures though architectural shapes are more abstract than a tree or a figure because of the associations these two imply.

In most of my work I try to poeticise the urban (built) environment and although feelings like sadness, loneliness, emptiness and melancholy can be negative feelings I try to turn them into something positive, attractive and even seductive. The paintings are based on the equilibrium and multiple use of planes, volumes and colours.

What are the techniques you use ?

I work only with brush and colour. My drawing is done with my brush and mainly is in oil as I find it to be the easiest material for experimenting with transparencies, tonal values, colour and form. Some of my paintings are more geometrical; in that case I find the precision of acrylic paint ideal to show the exact proportion of each plane and the spaces they define. Sometimes I am obsessed with the play of light and shadow upon surfaces of colour and texture, other times my fascination is in the geometry of a figure reassembled as a cubist abstract, and even beyond, to create ambiguities of surreal messages.

Whatever the subjects, I want my paintings to achieve lyricism, through either truth-telling or deceiving.

Vive la Différence, 1991, oil, 63.5 x 76 cm

Above: *The garden*, 1988, mixed media, 51 x 38 cm; Below: *Polykatikies, Athens*, 1992, oil, 51 x 40 cm

Confetti, 1992, oil, 24 x 16 cm

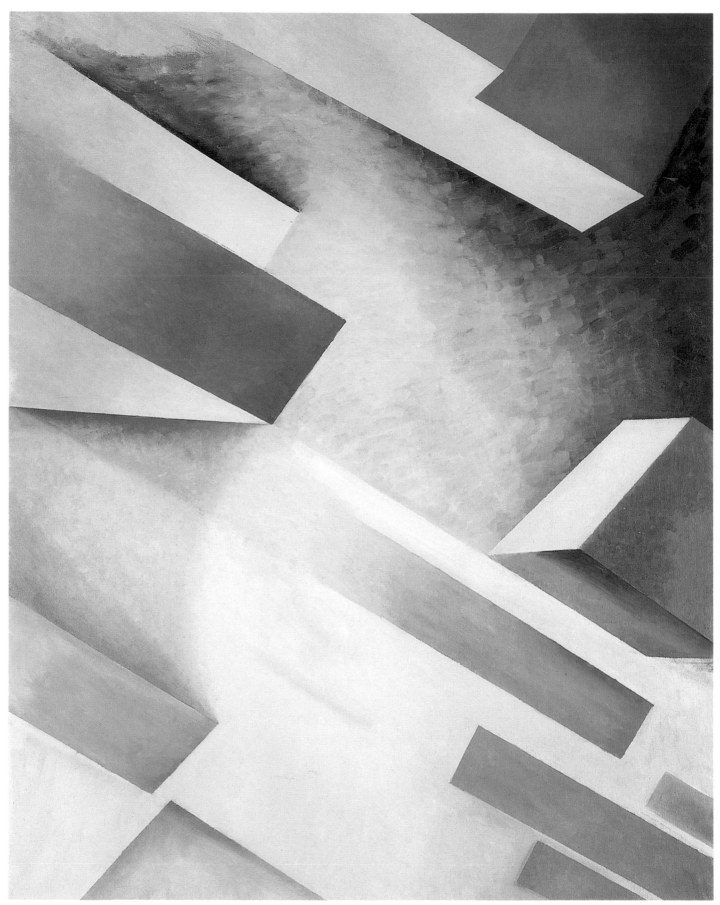

Composition 1, 1992, oil, 81 x 122 cm

Above: *Moving Planes* (detail), 1992, oil, 112 x 163 cm; Below: *Two Red*, 1992, oil, 122 x 61 cm

Above: *Fragments*, 1992, oil, 106 x 86 cm; Below: *The Meeting*, 1992, oil, 101 x 77 cm

Above: *Round City*, 1992, oil, 56 x 41 cm; Below: *Around the Light*, 1992, oil, 80 x 52 cm

XXII

Above: *Seaview*, 1992, oil, 122 x 82 cm; Below: *Desertion*, 1992, oil 58 x 43 cm
Opposite: *Cones and Squares*, 1992, oil, 81 x 122 cm

Above: *Whirlwind*, 1992, oil, 112 x 82 cm; Below: *Harmony*, 1992, oil, 53 x 33 cm
Previous spread: *Fields*, 1992, oil, 102 x 76 cm

Glass Highway, 1992, oil, 92 x 61 cm

Dreaming City, 1992, oil, 122 x 102 cm

Above: *Composition 2*, 1992, oil, 40 x 34 cm; Below: *Composition 3*, 1992, oil, 23 x 20 cm

Shapes in Space, 1992, oil, 122 x 91 cm

Light and Shade, 1992, oil, 92 x 60 cm

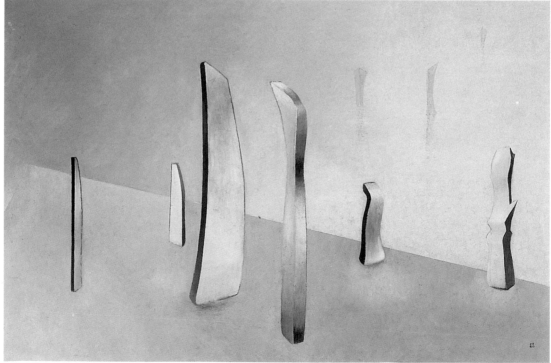

Above: *Awakening City*, 1991, oil; Below: *Waiting*, 1991, oil

Above: *Tall Red*, 1989, oil; Below: *Allotments,* 1990, oil

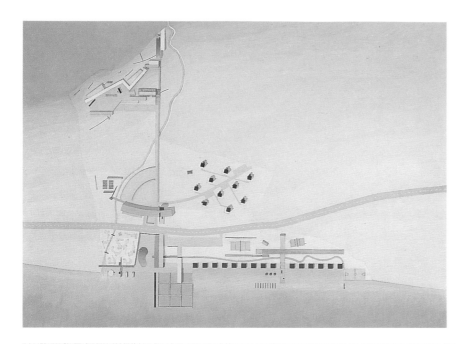

PAINTINGS FOR **OMA**

' . . . OMA is, to my knowledge, the only office to have artists as partners. They have celebrated congestion, artificiality, megalomania and optimism. Partly because of the collaboration of the two artists and their visual presentations of OMA's work, the office has been associated with mythical buildings which are more like monuments or sculptures than the throbbing, bustling conglomeration of disparate elements which make up the city as we know it . . . '
Jasia Reichard

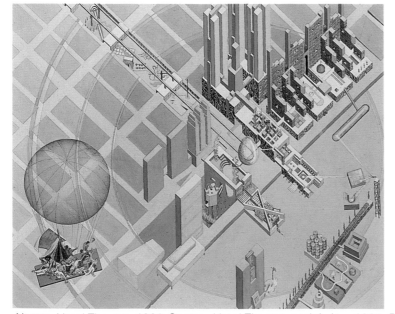

' . . . For Zoe Zenghelis, the role of the gentle artist, for it is she who makes the paintwork for much of both Elia's and Rem's drawings. But it is in this gentleness of colouration that the work of OMA can relate to more placid observers than, say, the work of the Krier brothers . . . ' *Peter Cook*

Above: *Hotel Therma, 1982*; Centre: *Hotel Therma, aerial view*, 1982, Below: *The Egg of Columbus Center*, 1975, mixed media on board

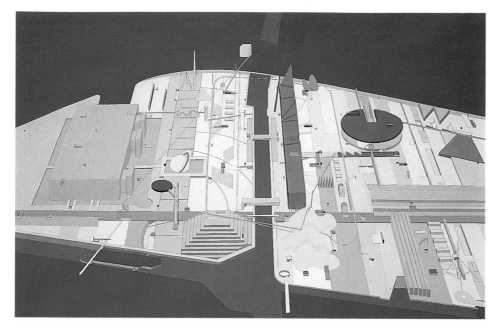

' . . . In La Villette we find in fact the pure exploitation of the metropolitan condition: density without architecture, the culture of the invisible congestion . . .' *L'Architecture d'aujourd'hui*

' . . . visionary projects such as a vast hotel, called Sphinx Hotel, because of its shape, for the middle of the north end of Times Square . . .' *Paul Goldberger, New York Times, 14/3/75, from 'Architectural Studies and Projects' exhibition, Museum of Modern Art, New York*

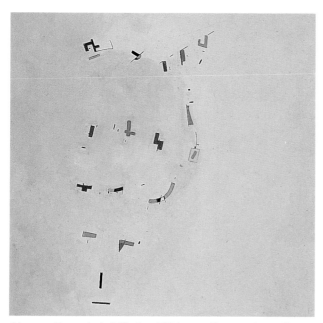

' . . . she presents the buildings as coloured boomerangs, an array of inexact geometric shapes dotted about a muted background . . .' *Jasia Reichard*

Above: *Parc de la Villette*, 1984, acrylic on paper; Centre: *Hotel Sphinx*, Elia and Zoe Zenghelis, 1975; Below: *Antiparos*, 1982, oil

Zoe **Zenghelis**

1938 Born in Athens, Greece
1956-60 Studied stage design and painting at Regent Street Polytechnic, London
1975 Founded OMA with Rem Koolhaas (architect), Madelon Vriesendorp (painter) and Elia Zenghelis (architect). Her contribution was mainly in the form of presentations, exhibitions and publications

Academic Positions

1984- Has been responsible for running the Colour Workshop at the Architectural Association, London. She has also been teaching at Plymouth Polytechnic, Brighton Polytechnic, Edinburgh University, USLA (USA) and Pomona State University (USA)
1991 Ran a 'Drawing and Painting' Summer School at the AA

Major Exhibitions

1974 'A Space, A Thousand Words', Royal College of Art, London
1979 ORA Gallery, Athens
1980 Nina Dausset Gallery, Paris
1981 Rosa Esman Gallery, New York
1982 Max Protetch Gallery, New York
1982 Camden Arts Centre, London
1985 Architectural Association, London
1987 Royal Academy Summer Exhibition, London
1989 ORA Gallery, Athens
1990 Long and Ryle, London
1991 Gallery K, London

1991 Represented Greece at FIWAL (Federation of International Women Artists in London)

Exhibitions of Architectural Paintings

1975 AICA Congress, Poland
1976/82 Institute for Architecture and Urban Studies, New York
1977 Time Life Building, New York (permanent exhibition)
1978 Museum of Modern Art, New York
1978 Stadelschula, Frankfurt
1980 Biennale, Venice
1980 Stedelijk Museum, Amsterdam
1981 'IBA Berlin 1984', Dortmund
1982 National Gallery, Greece
1982 Max Protetch Gallery, New York
1984 'Manspace' Building Centre, London
1987 Gemante Museum, The Hague
1988 National Gallery, Berlin

Bibliography

A Papadakis, C Cooke and A Benjamin *Deconstruction Omnibus*, Academy Editions, 1989
Architectural Design: Pop Architecture, Profile no 98, Academy Editions, London, 1992
Art & Design: New Museology, Profile no 22, Academy Editions, London, 1991
Zoe Zenghelis' work has appeared in numerous issues of *Art and Design* and *Architectural Design* throughout her career. Her paintings have also been published by *Lotus*, *L'Architecture d'aujourd' hui*, *Progressive Architecture*, *A+U*, *Building Design*, *Blueprint*, *Skyline* and *Casabella*

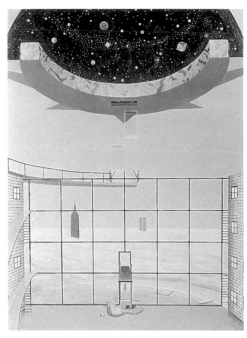

The Pool of the Sphinx, 1975, oil

ACKNOWLEDGEMENTS

I should like to express my gratitude first of all to Andreas Papadakis of Academy Editions for his support and enthusiasm throughout this project. Thanks are also due to Andrea Bettella and Jan Richter for designing this publication. Finally, I am especially indebted to Gallery K and the Architectural Association for putting on the exhibition. *Zoe Zenghelis*

Photographs by Radius and Rodney Todd-White

PATRICK CAULFIELD

Still Life: Maroochydore, *detail, 1980-81, acrylic on canvas, 152.4x152.4 cm (Leslie and Clodagh Waddington)*

Art & Design

Edited by Andreas Papadakis

PATRICK CAULFIELD
PAINTINGS 1963-1992

OPPOSITE: Lounge, *detail, 1989, acrylic on canvas, 289.5x205.7 cm (Waddington Galleries);*
ABOVE: Mural, *1982, 6x6 m, work in progress, (London Life Insurance, Bristol)*

A.D. ACADEMY EDITIONS · LONDON

Acknowledgements

This issue of *Art & Design* magazine is based on
PATRICK CAULFIELD: PAINTINGS 1963-1992
SERPENTINE GALLERY
Kensington Gardens, London W2 3XA, Telephone: 071 402 6075, Facsimile: 071 402 4103
24 November 1992 – 17 January 1993

We are grateful to the Serpentine Gallery for all their help in the production of this magazine and also to Marco Livingstone for providing the text; **Serpentine Gallery Staff** *Director* Julia Peyton-Jones; *Assistant Director* Andrea Schlieker; *Administrator/Development* Rebecca King Lassman; *Education Organiser* Vivien Ashley; *Press and Publicity* Julia Little; *Bookshop and Publications Managers* Gavin Everall and Ben Hillwood-Harris; *Exhibitions Assistant* Margaret Goddard; *Accounts* Anthea Packer; *Gallery Manager* Philip Monk; *Gallery Assistants* Amanda Bracken, Michael Gaughan, Deborah Hursefield, Sadie Murdoch, David Simpson

Lenders to the Exhibition Arts Council Collection, The South Bank Centre, London; The British Council; Collection Janet de Botton; Mrs T Chetwynd; Howard Hodgkin, London; Walker Art Gallery; Waddington Galleries; Leslie and Clodagh Waddington; National Westminster Bank plc; Private Collections

Photographic Credits AC Cooper; Prudence Cuming Associates Ltd; Sarah Knight; Tom Scott; Donald Southern; Rodney Todd-White and Son; Malcolm Varon; John Webb

Registered charity no 298890
The Serpentine Gallery Trust gratefully acknowledges financial support from the
Arts Council of Great Britain and Westminster City Council

COVER: Claret, *detail, 1992, acrylic on canvas, 61x79.2 cm (The artist, courtesy of Waddington Galleries)*
INSIDE FRONT COVER: After Lunch, *detail, 1975, acrylic on canvas, 244x213.4 cm (Trustees of the Tate Gallery)*
INSIDE BACK COVER: Town and Country, *detail, 1979, acrylic on canvas, 231.1x165.1 cm (Private Collection)*

EDITOR
Dr Andreas C Papadakis

EDITORIAL TEAM: Nicola Hodges, Vivian Constantinopoulos
DESIGN TEAM: Andrea Bettella (Senior Designer), Annamarie Uhr, Jan Richter
SUBSCRIPTIONS MANAGER: Mira Joka BUSINESS MANAGER: Sheila de Vallée

First published in Great Britain in 1992 by *Art & Design* an imprint of the
ACADEMY GROUP LTD, 42 LEINSTER GARDENS, LONDON W2 3AN
MEMBER OF THE VCH PUBLISHING GROUP

ISBN: 1 85490 180 X

Printed and bound in Singapore

Contents

Model of set and costumes for Party Games, *1984, ballet by Michael Corder at the Royal Opera House, Covent Garden*

ART & DESIGN PROFILE No 27

PATRICK CAULFIELD
PAINTINGS 1963-1992

The Atrium Carpet, *1992, designed by Patrick Caulfield, manufactured by Heuga (UK) Ltd and commissioned by the British Council for their Manchester Headquarters*

ANDREA SCHLIEKER
FOREWORD

For the past three decades Patrick Caulfield's work has been devoted to the genres of interior and still life. His acute observations of mundane, everyday surroundings are laced with a subversive sense of humour and irony. Yet unlike his historical antecedents – from early Netherlandish painting to classic Cubism – Caulfield's highly stylised renditions of familiar pub, restaurant and domestic scenes, can be read as icons of the artificiality of the modern world.

Caulfield is a master of the ordinary, prosaic and unheroic side of urban life. Although he single-mindedly concentrates on places of conviviality, his paintings exude a detached and ultra-cool atmosphere. Caulfield's bars and cafés are almost always conspicuously devoid of human presence. A switched-on lamp, an empty glass and a plate full of food seem to make this absence even more poignant.

Caulfield trained at the Royal College of Art in the early 1960s at a time when Warhol had just painted his first Campbell soup can and Lichtenstein was experimenting with his appropriations of the comic strip. Like the early Pop artists, Caulfield was strongly influenced by the strategies of advertising and the language of contemporary design. In both style and subject-matter his paintings echo and explore the relationship between fine art and mass culture.

After the formal simplicity of his works from the 1960s, Caulfield introduces paintings of increasing spatial and stylistic complexity at the end of the next decade. Here he confidently engineers collisions with conventional 'good taste' by juxtaposing bright, clashing colours with busy patterns and different painting styles. Caulfield has been moving continually towards more radical solutions in his paintings, and the bold compositions of his most recent works are eloquent testimony to the success of this endeavour. The emphasis on objects and textures of the familiar urban landscape continues in these paintings, but the rigour of their construction – mainly expressed through a formalisation of imagined light – the assured and impeccable deployment of colour, gives them an extraordinary vitality and freshness, that confirms Caulfield's position at the forefront of contemporary painting.

This exhibition at the Serpentine Gallery, which brings together paintings from the 1960s to the present day, is the first opportunity to see Caulfield's work on a major scale since his retrospective at the Walker Art Gallery in Liverpool and the Tate Gallery in London eleven years ago. On behalf of the Serpentine Gallery I would like to thank all the private and public lenders who generously agreed to part with their work for the duration of this exhibition. Waddington Galleries, in particular Sarah Tooley, were helpful in supplying us with the necessary information to secure the loans. We are delighted that Dr Andreas Papadakis of Academy Editions has agreed to publish our Caulfield catalogue as part of *Art & Design* magazine, and are grateful to him as well as to Edwina Sassoon for making this collaboration possible. Marco Livingstone has long been established as the foremost authority on Patrick Caulfield's work, and I would like to thank him most warmly for not only writing an excellent essay for this publication, but also for his informed advice and support throughout the preparatory stages of the exhibition. Lastly, our thanks are due to Patrick Caulfield, whose thoughtful and attentive engagement with the exhibition and its selection have resulted in a coherent survey of his work, which we are proud to present at the Serpentine Gallery.

MARCO LIVINGSTONE
PATRICK CAULFIELD: A TEXT FOR SILENT PICTURES

For a long time after I first came upon Patrick Caulfield's work I admired it above all for the intelligence of its construction and its complex relationship to other art, for its pictorial wit, for its eloquent balance between linear qualities and emotive colour and for its formal resolution. These strengths are certainly recognised by his fellow artists: he is rare in being admired equally by representational and abstract artists, by traditionalists and conceptualists. Yet now I think that what moves me most about his art is the variety of subtle ways in which all these characteristics serve in a general sense to embody human frailty and more specifically to bring into focus the dilemmas associated with the creative act. The kinds of questions that must nag at every artist who has chosen to carry on working in a medium increasingly at variance with the 'progress' of culture – why paint? what to paint? how to paint? – in Caulfield's work take on an almost desperate edge. Yet his sense of humour and plainspeaking visual language save his art from pomposity, just as the clarity of his pictorial conceptions and vividness of his colour schemes guarantee an optimism and vibrancy of effect even when the scene is suggestive of bleakness or ennui.

It's a wonder that Caulfield has completed as many paintings as he has over the past 30 years, no matter how slow and considered his production may appear in relation to that of most of his contemporaries. Being of a melancholic and contemplative nature, everything in his measured and silent art would appear to conspire against action. Consider his attraction to scenes of conviviality, the displays of food and drink in intimate but apparently unpopulated restaurant interiors captured with an eerie stillness. The most prevalent images in his recent pictures are of pipes and of glasses of wine, whisky or beer in smoke-filled pub interiors. The tumblers, goblets and wine glasses have the greatest detail lavished on them, so that they look more enticing and more fully in focus than any of the other elements in the picture. We find ourselves staring at their contents with the same longing and absent-minded fixation that we might well experience when such a glass of alcohol is placed before us, regardless of whether it represents a well-earned pleasure or a dangerous temptation, a moment of relaxation or an invitation to temporary oblivion. The pipes are perhaps there simply as a source for the smoke we imagine as proper to the airless atmosphere of these locales; Caulfield is a good host and he wants to make sure we feel relaxed and in our element. Or perhaps the pipes function as images of male friendship and tolerance, a sign of social interaction. They're certainly not autobiographical signs; I've never seen him smoke.

Judging from his pictures, Caulfield's attention seems as easily distracted as that of the reluctant office-worker, the comic-strip character Bristow, whose ingenuity at avoiding work has so consistently amused him that he has become a good friend of the cartoonist responsible for his invention, Frank Dickens. This is not to say that Caulfield is work-shy, only that, like most of us, he must have to find ways of pushing himself to get things done. There is an undeniable paradox, after all, about having to lock oneself away in a room all day in order to produce pictures that hint of human interaction. Under the circumstances there is something inevitable about the mood of sad reverie or wistful longing that often engulfs Caulfield's pictures; one gets the impression he would rather put the brushes away and step into this other world himself, and that the act of making a representation thus becomes a form of compulsive daydreaming.

The solitude and longueurs of life in the artist's work-place, the studio, are often displaced metaphorically in Caulfield's art by allusion to the banal circumstances that circumscribe all our lives. His pictures are full of images suggesting distraction bordering at times on a trance-like state. When we are asked to place ourselves in the position of an office worker, as in *After Work* 1977, it is at the low ebb of energy at the end of the day when the in-tray has finally been emptied and the typewriter pushed aside, and we are free at last simply to gaze out over the skyline of the city at dusk. Relaxing our inhibitions, we find ourselves noticing the beautiful shapes formed by the shadows cast by the objects that have bedevilled us all day; or we gaze with irrational intensity at the stylised pattern of an artificial wood-grained surface, as we struggle to concentrate our thoughts, as a way of shaking ourselves out of an exhausted stupor.

In a related canvas, *Office Party* 1977, the most persuasively true element is that of the enticing view through the window of the top of an ecclesiastical building under a limpid blue sky at dusk. The evidence, however, suggests that this is perhaps no more than a photographic image printed on an alluring travel poster, since it is unlikely that an office party would take place opposite Spoleto Cathedral. A few glasses of Italian wine – those distinctly shaped green bottles clearly hold 75cl of verdicchio, the dark ones probably chianti – might sufficiently blur the distinction between fantasy and reality to persuade us, momentarily, that we have been whisked away from our prosaic existence into a never-ending perpetual holiday, where all we have to do is sit in the sun and make ourselves quietly merry with drink. Those dreadfully stale peanuts at the bottom of the bowl will soon jolt us back to the here-and-now, but the illusion is pleasant while it lasts and no less real for existing only in our minds.

Similar moments of escapist fantasy punctured by dull reality have consistently been called forth by Caulfield's paintings. There are recurring instances of normally banal views transformed into something magical by unexpectedly luscious conjunctions of coloured forms and natural phenomena, as with the arrangement of minimalist chimneys against a shrill red sky in *View of the Rooftops* 1965, and frequent forays into picture-postcard landscapes and exotic locations, from the Mediterranean seascapes of *Santa Margherita Ligure* and *View of the Bay* in 1964 to a French river scene in colours taken from an Australian postcard in *Still Life: Maroochydore* in 1980-81. There are abundant instances, too, of the getting-away-from-it-all interiors of more closed-in holiday homes of the kind that we could easily emulate with the aid of a few copies of *House and Garden* or *The World of Interiors* and a visit or two to the local DIY shop to collect suitably authentic architectural details; *Inside a Weekend Cabin* and *Inside a Swiss Chalet,* both painted in 1969, typically present antiseptic modern spaces made 'characterful' by the none-too-subtle intrusion of such corny features as milkmaid's stools and high-backed wooden chairs with heart-shaped openings.

These first full-scale pictures of holiday rooms led, in turn, to numerous views of restaurant interiors defining a kind of sanitised foreignness. Beginning with *Bistro* 1970 and *Tandoori Restaurant* 1971 and continuing through the elaborate pretence of Swissness of *After Lunch* 1975 and *Still Life: Maroochydore*'s gastronomic display – a sure-fire recipe for international indigestion – Caulfield has reminded us mercilessly of our insatiable appetites for such culinary excursions as a means of reassuring ourselves of our cosmopolitan sophistication. Yet we know very well that such interludes offer only a brief respite from dreary routine: the credit card symbols at the entrance to *Paradise Bar* 1974, for instance, remind us not only about how small and how temporary this carefree oasis really is, but also that like everything else it eventually has to be paid for.

Caulfield's art is rich in terms of its candid and precise observations of the way we live, but he is no social realist – although it is interesting that when he was asked to define Pop Art in 1991, on the occasion of the Royal Academy survey exhibition in which his work was featured, he described it as 'Social Realism without emotion'. His overriding concern has been to unmask human behaviour, and in particular the ways in which we delude ourselves, and in that sense he is more of a psychologist than a documentarist. It just happens that he prefers to drive the points home, literally, by reference to the precise circumstances of our lives, consumerist and internationally confused in outlook, at the end of the 20th century.

However reluctant Caulfield has been to align himself with Pop Art, his work has shared fundamental features with that of other artists associated with the movement: a preference for anonymity of technique in opposition to blatantly self-expressive brushwork, references in his procedures to nonartistic sources (including sign-painting, advertising

Girl in a Doorway, *1969, oil on canvas, 274.3x182.9 cm (Ulster Museum)*

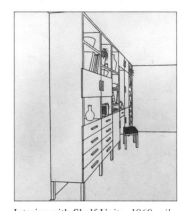

Interior with Shelf Units, *1969, oil on canvas, 213.4x182.9 cm (Waddington Galleries)*

Window at Night, *1969, oil on canvas, 213.4x152.4 cm (Private Collection)*

and children's colouring books), a sense of humour, a wilful banality in his choice of motifs and an interest in mass taste and kitsch.

There are, of course, many distinctions to be made between Caulfield's approach and that of his more aggressively Pop colleagues, particularly in America. Lichtenstein, with whom he is most easily compared stylistically because of the graphic treatment of images in black outline and flat, bright colours, based his methods self-evidently on the contemporary printed comic strips that served also as the source of his blatant teenage imagery; Caulfield, on the other hand, has always avoided the trappings of youth culture and refused to disguise the hand-made quality of his paintings. While Warhol focussed on images of celebrity and brand-name consumption, Caulfield dignified familiar but forlorn motifs and allowed only the rare intrusion of an unidentified figure. Where Rosenquist or Wesselmann emblazoned motifs from contemporary advertising onto towering canvases the size of billboards, Caulfield made reference to generalised classes of objects and slightly out-of-date items poignantly deprived of fashionability, and he deliberately avoided the monumental effects of gigantism, wishing instead to work within the European tradition of easel painting; there is a consistent and pure logic to his choice of scale in relation to the objects he represents, as a result of which he expands the size of his working surface only when dealing with the architectural subjects that demand such treatment.

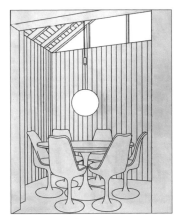

Dining Recess, *1972, acrylic on canvas, 274.5x213.5 cm (Arts Council Collection, The South Bank Centre, London)*

Like most Pop artists, Caulfield adopted an inexpressive technique as a student in the early 1960s partly in defiance of the gestural procedures then favoured both by the Abstract Expressionists and other abstract painters and by figurative artists such as Frank Auerbach and Leon Kossoff, and also as a retort to the tentative quality of Slade School figurative painting, where every mark is tremulously measured against the motif. Yet he resisted the temptation to rely on mechanical procedures such as photo-screen printing or to incorporate found printed images in the form of collage, painting his pictures exclusively by hand and from 1964 availing himself of screenprinting only as an efficient graphic method for the dissemination of his designs as editioned prints. At a basic level, Caulfield simply wanted his work to look as effortless and emphatic as possible, countering the anxiety implicit in heavily worked surfaces or hesitant brushmarks with a continuous surface that would give the impression of having been arrived at through a procedure as prosaic as that of a house-painter. His pictures of 1963-64 have the surface quality of doors decorated with gloss paint; his works from the mid-1960s to the mid-1970s, painted first in artist's oils and from the early 1970s in acrylic, could be likened more to the matt surfaces of walls coated in emulsion. Caulfield's greatest regret is that he could not get the density of colour he required with a single coat of paint. The apparent effortlessness is, in the end, of course an illusion, a way of covering his tracks and of denying the difficulties of picture-making which he encountered to the same degree as any other artist.

Still Life: Maroochydore, *1980-81, acrylic on canvas, 152.4x152.4 cm (Leslie and Clodagh Waddington)*

Fish and Sandwich, *1984, acrylic on canvas, 76.2x111.8 cm (Saatchi Collection)*

The anonymous surfaces favoured by Caulfield as early as 1961, when he was a young postgraduate student at the Royal College of Art, have more in common with old-fashioned shop signs than with the modern industrial world. His choice of a humble household enamel gloss paint as a coating over the unyielding surface of hardboard immediately stripped the paintings of selfconscious artiness; a disturbing marriage of intentionally crude effect with breezy confidence, they present themselves blatantly as outworn clichés as a means of dislodging the more insidious clichés of expressive modern painting. The mechanisms by which Caulfield divested painting of over-dramatised emotion are particularly clear in *Greece Expiring on the Ruins of Missolonghi after Delacroix* 1963, his solution to the final year project set by the Royal College for a transcription of an Old Master painting. Rather than imitating the techniques of its source or abstracting the formal values of its composition, he invented the colours from a black-and-white reproduction and brought out the salient features of the imagery as a way of exaggerating the qualities it shares with political propaganda posters. The Romanticism of the source survives this process of conceptualisation. Emotion is not banished altogether, but transformed into characteristics that can be measured and assimilated more dispassionately: image, colour, shape and outline.

The romantic and the exotic continued to feature prominently in the imagery of Caulfield's paintings of the 1960s, such as *Still Life with Dagger* 1963, *The Artist's Studio* 1964 and *Still Life with Necklace* 1964, all of which include Islamic metalwork and Turkish pottery as still-life elements. In works such as these and *View of the Ruins* 1964, Caulfield presents his art, with self-deprecating irony, as heir to the Orientalism for which there was such a taste in 19th-century Britain. However far he has gone in expunging the picturesque qualities of his sources by reshaping the motifs in a flat graphic idiom and by removing them from their customary context into an austere and highly formalised setting, the suspicion remains that he has more than a sneaking liking for the exotic himself. How could it be otherwise, when a major impetus towards his mature style was the ancient Minoan frescoes that he encountered during visits to Crete in 1961 and 1963? Characteristically he was guided not so much by the original frescoes themselves as by their reproductions in the form of postcards, to which black outlines had been added as a means of strengthening the divisions between different areas of flat colour. Far from rejecting tradition, Caulfield seeks to salvage it by taking it up in its most debased form and making it new again.

Forecourt, *1975, acrylic on canvas, 274.3x243.8 cm (Private Collection)*

The *Artist's Eye* exhibition selected by Caulfield for the National Gallery in 1986 was deeply revealing of the predilections at work in his own paintings – rather than necessarily of his passions in the history of art – and of his courting of the obvious as a means of subverting expectations. The obvious in this situation did not mean plucking the best-known masterpieces from the collection, as other artists had done when selecting their exhibitions for the National Gallery, but on the contrary in presenting works that it many cases had been little noticed but that conformed to broad categories in the history of painting: landscapes, seascapes and cityscapes; interiors and other architectural settings with incidental figures, and figure scenes in interiors; portraits; and still lifes. These, of course, are very like the categories to which Caulfield's own paintings have corresponded. It is easy to understand his attraction to particular pictures because of the evident relationship between them and his own works, as in his choice of *The Interior of the Grote Kerk at Harlem* by the 17th-century Dutch painter Pieter Saenredam, a precisely ordered and light-filled architectural view that provides an admirable precedent for Caulfield's equally serene interiors. The two still lifes he selected from the many available to him, by the Dutch 17th-century painter Jan Van de Velde and the French 19th-century artist Philippe Rousseau, have in common not only motifs that have featured in Caulfield's paintings – glasses of wine and oysters – but also a focussing of light and precision of technique on these strategically selected elements within otherwise vaguely suggested atmospheric spaces.

Pottery, *1969, oil on canvas, 213.5x152.5 cm (Trustees of the Tate Gallery)*

The presentation of light as a material substance, a concern for atmosphere in creating mood and the directing of the spectator's vision by means of variable degrees of finish – a characteristic of Caulfield's art that emerged in the mid-1970s – are, in fact, to be found also in many of the other pictures selected by him in *The Artist's Eye,* including 19th-century landscapes and tavern or cafe scenes by Adriaen Brouwer and Edouard Manet. Several of the portraits and interiors – including works as diverse as those by or ascribed to three painters of the early Renaissance, Vincenzo Catena, Dieric Bouts and Piero di Cosimo – feature views through windows that function as pictures within the picture, a device often used by Caulfield. Two courtyard scenes by the 17th-century Dutch painter Pieter de Hoogh, and Velázquez's *Kitchen Scene with Christ in the House of Martha and Mary,* highlight a related strategy that Caulfield has employed to particular effect in interiors such as *Forecourt* 1975 and *Dining/Kitchen/Living* 1980: that of a distant view as a spatial counterpoint and secondary focus to the primary event presented in the foreground of the picture.

Caulfield's *Artist's Eye* exhibition tells us much about the way that he goes about constructing his own pictures, rather than about the historical sources for his art as a whole, since in terms of famous names or stylistic coherence it provides only fragmentary and inconclusive evidence for his own taste. The influences on him, which I discussed in some detail in my catalogue essay for Caulfield's retrospective in 1981 at the Walker Art Gallery and Tate Gallery, were much closer to home in the 20th century. They include, in particular, two major modernist painters for whom Caulfield has painted explicit homages: the Spanish Cubist Juan Gris (*Portrait of Juan Gris* 1963) and the Belgian Surrealist René Magritte (*The Mysterious Suspicion – After Magritte* 1974). He has also drawn sustenance from

Fernand Léger, both stylistically in his use of flat areas of colour bordered in black outline and in his presentation of motifs as quasi-symbolic 'object types'. The decorative qualities and full-blooded, evocative colour of Matisse's work have also left their mark, particularly on Caulfield's interiors, which – like Matisse's *Red Interior* of 1911 – are generally drenched in a single intense hue. In these plaintively still and empty pictures of architecture, the atmospheres of which are paradoxically heightened by the exaggerated and stylised depiction of shafts of intense light and deep shadow, he has revealed a respectful sympathy for the paintings of the American Edward Hopper. More tangentially, there are references to the work of other mainstream modernists, often laced with irony, as in his reshaping of Raoul Dufy's Mediterranean harbour scenes as picture-postcard views and in his allusions to the geometric forms of Mondrian or to the monochrome expanses of Minimalism.

Still Life with Dagger, *1963, oil on board, 121.5x122 cm (Trustees of the Tate Gallery)*

Caulfield has spent his life as an artist dodging other people's expectations and confounding his own habits, wary of being trapped into a successful formula even if it is one of his own making. Having stripped down his pictorial language to the bare essentials of black descriptive outline over monochrome grounds, he began in the mid-1970s to recomplicate his pictures. At first it was sufficient for his purposes to interrupt the seamless monochrome surface with a passage containing a variety of other colours, as in *Forecourt* 1975, or to puncture his conventions of representation more dramatically by painting selected elements in an illusionistically detailed technique. This solution could be effected quite simply, as with the rendering of the flowers in a pair of small pictures painted in 1975, *Still Life: Mother's Day* and *Still Life: Father's Day*. Alternatively, the deception may be as complex and sustained as that of the Swiss view featured in *After Lunch* 1975, which on first sight is easily taken to signify a view through a window but which one subsequently realises can represent nothing more than a photographic counterfeit for reality pressed flat against a freestanding screen. This sham, in turn, is almost instantly revealed as a double-bluff or even triple-bluff: the image may look photographic, but closer scrutiny reveals it to be hand-painted, and as soon as we can congratulate ourselves on our deciphering of the room's layout we have to remind ourselves that the whole of the scene is nothing but an elaborate simulation of actual space onto the surface of the canvas.

Smokeless Coal Fire, *1969, oil on canvas, 152.4x91.4 cm (Whitworth Art Gallery)*

By the late 1970s Caulfield's work, once so elegantly restrained, was becoming characterised by a *horror vacui*. The sophisticated and skilful layering of pictorial conventions even in small canvases such as *Still Life: Autumn Fashion* 1978 lends them an extraordinary intensity and mystery. We are presented with a multiplicity of systems of representation, with different types of illusion, and with conflicting signals for light and space that would lead us up the garden path if we could actually see through the imaginary window. In spite, however, of this glut of visual information we can somehow still believe in the image as a whole as a sign for reality. In one of the most imposing of these canvases, *Town and Country* 1979, every patch of the surface is rendered in *trompe-l'oeil* detail or covered in dazzling patterns that clash violently against one another. The ambiguities are more complex and more subtle than ever before, focussed particularly on the elaborate ploy of a floor-to-ceiling recessed mural as a counterfeit outdoor view. There is so much going in purely perceptual terms that it is easy to forget to question what the scene as a whole might signify. Are we at the end of the working day, approaching six pm, cocktail time? Or can we extrapolate from the imagery, especially from the conjunction of dusk with the dying leaves on a huge and ancient tree, a more metaphorical reading of the image as a comment on encroaching old age?

In *Still Life: Maroochydore* 1980-81, Caulfield humorously presented the range of pictorial options as a kind of smorgasbord of style, literally giving us some of the available choices 'on a plate'. The scope was limited for developing further such copious complexity, and it must therefore have been with some relief in 1982 that he was able to revert to a more stylised conception of a still-life subject for his largest painting to date: a painting measuring 20 feet by 20 feet commissioned by the London Life insurance company as a focal point for the entrance hall of their headquarters in Bristol. Executed entirely by the artist himself on 12 pieces of hardboard, it is not an ordinary mural but a giant picture, its identity as such emphasised by its heavy frame. A thick black outline, as in his earlier work, establishes a strong formal structure while transforming 'abstract' shapes into emblematic representations. Each item, though ordinary in itself, has a particular significance in terms of Bristol's historic trading links and industries; the decanter and window (invisible to the eye but implicit in the reflection of the carafe) represent sherry and glass, the pipe tobacco, the curtain and tablecloth cotton. The timber industry is alluded to not only by the representation of wood within the picture but also by the frame, its apparently crude construction calling to mind primitive art and by association the slave trade of Bristol's past. The schematic representation in the upper right of the Egyptian-style tower of the Clifton Suspension Bridge provides a key: the painting as a whole is like a hieroglyph, a picture relating a specific message.

Black and White Flower Piece, *1963, oil on board, 122x122 cm (Trustees of the Tate Gallery)*

The compression of imagery and complexity of colour scheme and pictorial conventions still evident in Caulfield's most ambitious paintings of the early 1980s, such as *Wine Bar* 1983, and even in smaller canvases such as *Candle-lit Dinner* 1981-82, gradually gave way again to a far more minimal conception. The series of new paintings that he presented at Waddington Galleries in 1989 genuinely perplexed some of his longstanding admirers. The signature style of flat images outlined in black was virtually nowhere in evidence, replaced instead by broad expanses of sometimes loosely brushed backgrounds punctuated by circular, ovoid and quasi-rectangular coloured shapes and by motifs picked out in a highly illusionistic technique. There is no longer any pretence about presenting a continuous expanse of space. Instead the fragmented points of interest – in the form both of persuasively volumetric and realistically rendered representations and of flat graphic signs for light – float in an indeterminate space or against an unmodulated monochrome ground. The emphasis in these works on the surface, and their denial of pictorial depth, brings them much closer to the qualities of Caulfield's work of the early 1960s, though with the benefit of the technical and stylistic refinements of the intervening years.

In certain of the new pictures the most desirable-looking element, the one on which Caulfield has lavished the greatest sleight-of-hand in terms of detail, is placed so high on the canvas that it is almost impossible for the viewer to see. Such is the case in *Buffet* 1987, where an image of a decorative porcelain plate is tantalisingly dangled just out of reach. The promised pleasure is denied to us, just as the artist has perversely forbidden himself from making his most expert handwork more immediately visible. In other pictures such as *Patio* 1988, the enjoyment elicited by the patterns of raked paint is similarly frustrated: not only can we not act on our natural inclination to touch, we are left forever wondering about the original appearance of this surface before it was completely hidden under successive layers of coloured paint. When I asked him why he chose to circumvent the final attainment of gratification in these ways, his reply was typically terse: 'Well, life's like that.'

As a consequence of these various strategies, Caulfield has retained his capacity to surprise while sacrificing none of his artistic identity. The more contrary the means, the more the pictures seem to ring true. Without explaining my reaction in any detail, I congratulated him on the new paintings shortly after the exhibition had taken place, saying I thought they were more like him than almost anything he had previously done. He looked genuinely horrified. 'But *that*', he exclaimed, 'is the *opposite* of what I'm trying to do!'

Santa Margherita Ligure, *1964 (destroyed), oil on board, 122x244 cm (Bryan Morrison)*

13

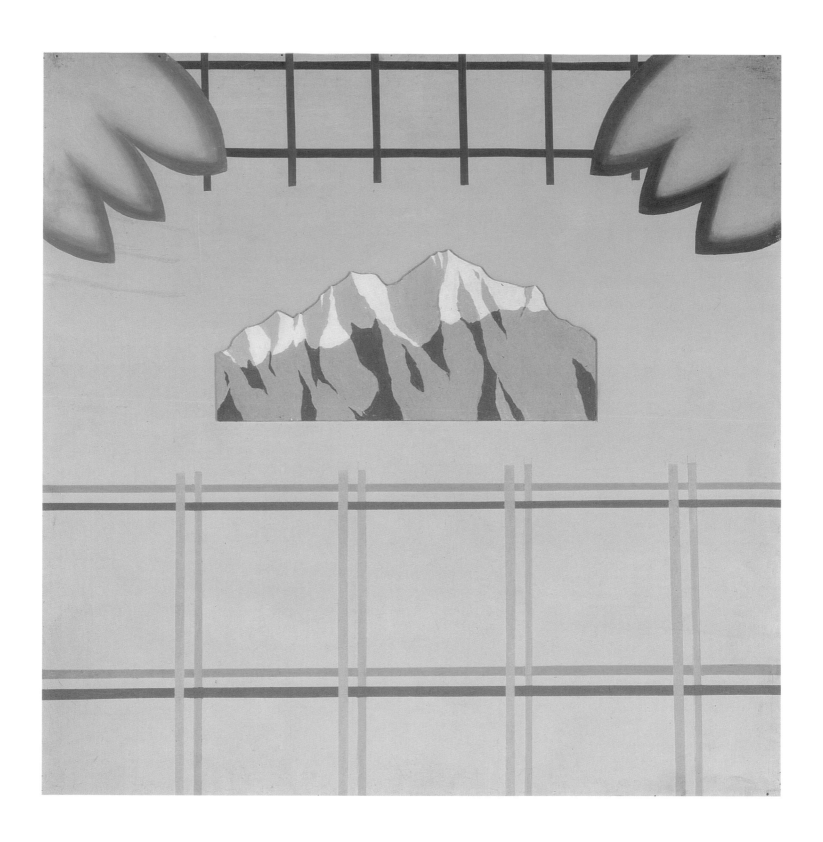

Leaving Arabia, *1961, oil and collage on board, 121.9x121.9 cm (Private Collection)*

Upright Pines, *1961, oil on board, 121.9x121.9 cm (Private Collection)*

Bottle and Drape, *1962, oil on hardboard, 122x122 cm (Private Collection)*

Landscape with Birds, *1963, oil on board, 122x122 cm (Private Collection)*

Greece Expiring on the Ruins of Missolonghi, *1963, oil on board, 152.4x121.9 cm (Trustees of the Tate Gallery)*

ABOVE: Vase of Flowers, *1963, oil on board, 121.9x121.9 cm (Trustees of the Tate Gallery);*
BELOW: Portrait of Juan Gris, *1963, gloss paint on hardboard, 121.9x121.9 cm (Private Collection)*

ABOVE: View of the Bay, *1964, oil on board, 183x122 cm (Collection Centro de Arte Moderna/Fundacao Calouste Gulbenkian);*
BELOW: Still Life on a Table, *1964, oil on board, 123x152.5 cm (Private Collection)*

ABOVE: Red and White Still Life, *1964, oil on board, 160x213.4 cm (Private Collection);*
BELOW: Corner of the Studio, *1964, oil on board, 91.4x213.4 cm (Leslie and Clodagh Waddington)*

Still Life with Bottle, Glass and Drape, *1964, oil on board, 157.5x152.4 cm (Private Collection)*

ABOVE: The Artist's Studio, *1964, oil on board, 91.4x213.4 cm (Arts Council Collection);*
BELOW: Perfume Jar, *1964, oil on canvas, 91.4x213.4 cm (Waddington Galleries)*

ABOVE: Still Life with Jug and Bottle, *1965, oil on hardboard, 91.4x213.3 cm (Private Collection);*
BELOW: Earthenware, *1966, oil on canvas, 91.4x152.4 cm (Private Collection)*

Stained Glass Window, *1967, oil on canvas, 213.4x121.9 cm (Waddington Galleries)*

ABOVE: Bend in the Road, *1967, oil on canvas, 122x216 cm (Private Collection);*
BELOW: Large Storage Jars, *1967, oil on canvas, 121.9x213.4cm (Private Collection)*

ABOVE: Still Life on a Checked Table, *1968, oil on canvas, 91.4x152.4 cm (The artist, courtesy of Waddington Galleries);*
BELOW: Guitar and Rug, *1968, oil on canvas, 91.4x152.6 cm (Hirshhorn Museum and Sculpture Garden,*
Smithsonian Institution, Washington DC, gift of Joseph H Hirshhorn, 1980)

Italian Girl, *1968, oil on canvas, 213.4x152.4 cm (National Museum of Wales)*

Lit Window, *1969, oil on canvas, 213x154 cm (Private Collection)*

Inside a Swiss Chalet, 1969, oil on canvas, 213.5x152.5 cm (Waddington Galleries)

Inside a Weekend Cabin, *1969, oil and acrylic on canvas, 274.4x183 cm (City of Manchester Art Galleries)*

O Helen, I Roam my Room, *1970, gouache, 43.8x37.5 cm (Private Collection)*

Villa Plage, *1970, oil on canvas, 365.8x152.4 cm (Waddington Galleries)*

Bistro, *1970, oil on canvas, 274.3x182.8 cm (Sydney and Frances Lewis)*

Tandoori Restaurant, *1971, oil on canvas, 274.3x152.4 cm (Wolverhampton Art Gallery)*

Interior with Room Divider, 1971, acrylic and oil on canvas, 213.4x182.8 cm (Private Collection)

Girl on a Terrace, *1971, oil on canvas, 213.4x152.4 cm (Private Collection)*

Vineyard, *1971, acrylic on canvas, 274.3x213.4 cm (Private Collection)*

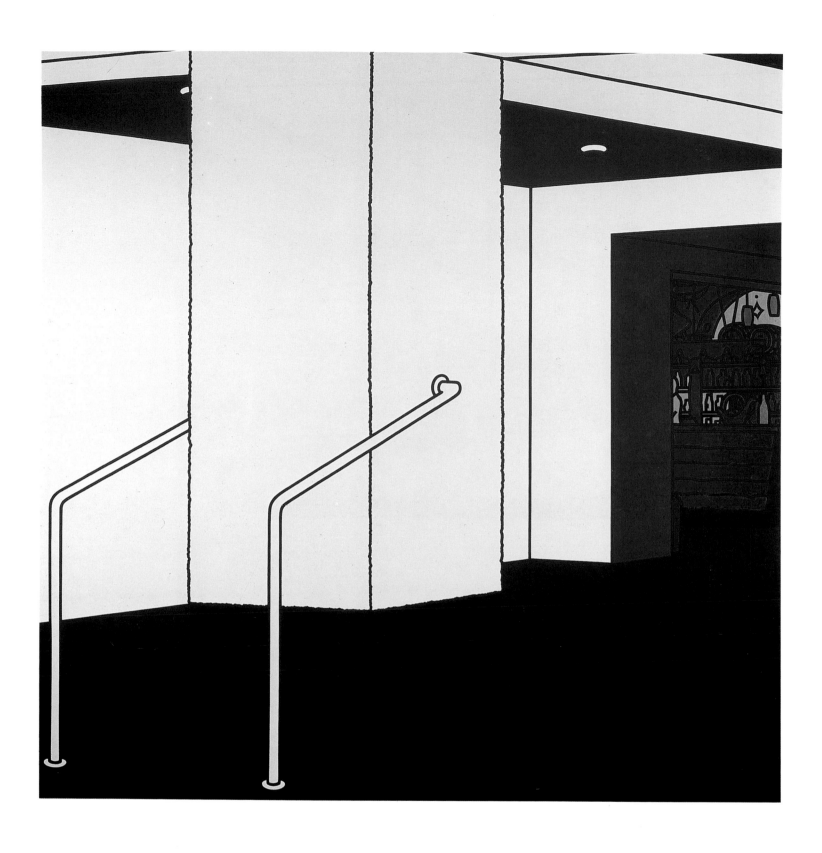

Foyer, 1973, acrylic on canvas, 213.4x213.4 cm (Saatchi Collection)

ABOVE: Cafe Interior: Afternoon, *1973, oil on canvas, 214.6x214.6 cm (Private Collection);*
BELOW: Inner Office, *1973, acrylic on canvas, 213.4x213.4 cm (Sandy Rotman)*

Paradise Bar, 1974, acrylic on canvas, 274.5x213.5 cm (Virginia Museum of Fine Arts, Richmond, Virginia)

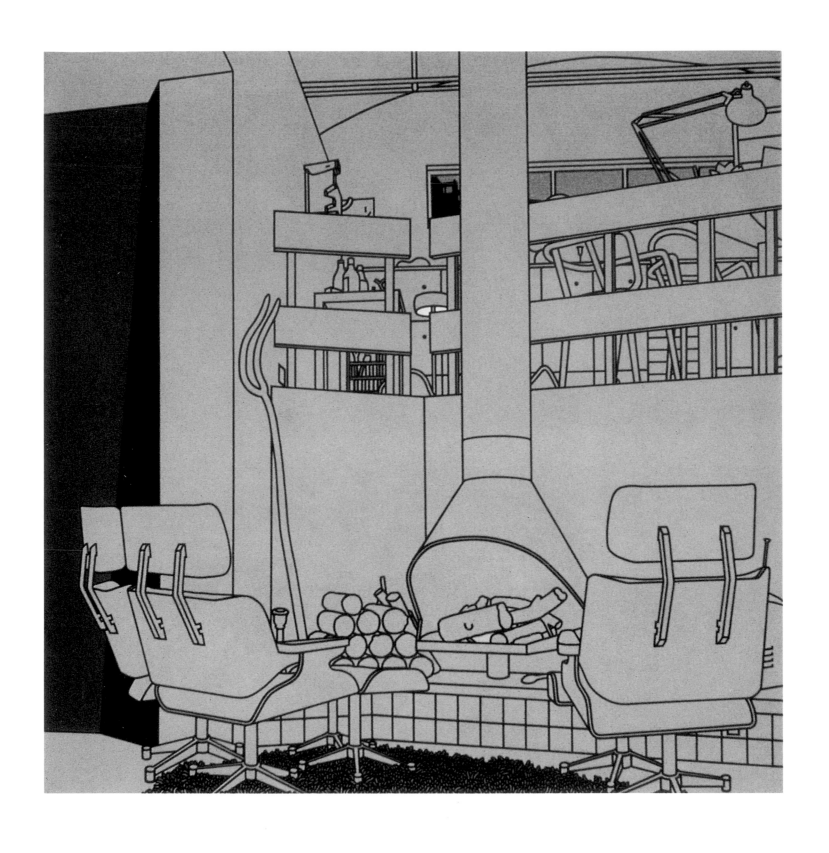

In My Room, 1974, acrylic on canvas, 274.5x274.5 cm (Collection of the Virginia Museum of Fine Arts, gift of Sydney and Frances Lewis)

The Mysterious Suspicion – After Magritte, *1974, acrylic on canvas, 274.3x152.4 cm*
(Collection of the Virginia Museum of Fine Arts, gift of Sydney and Frances Lewis)

Entrance, *1975, acrylic on canvas, 304.8x213.4 cm (Sydney and Frances Lewis)*

Sun Lounge, *1975, acrylic on canvas, 304.8x213.4 cm (Private Collection)*

Still Life: Mother's Day, *1975, acrylic on canvas, 61x91.5 cm (Leslie and Clodagh Waddington)*

Still Life: Father's Day, *1975, acrylic on canvas, 91.4x76.2 cm (Private Collection)*

After Lunch, 1975, acrylic on canvas, 244x213.4 cm (Trustees of the Tate Gallery)

Study of Roses, *1976, acrylic on canvas, 91.4x76.1 cm (National Westminster Bank plc)*

After Work, 1977, acrylic on canvas, 76.2x91.4 cm (Carol Kroch-Rhodes)

ABOVE: Office Party, *1977, acrylic on canvas, 61x91.5 cm (Leslie and Clodagh Waddington);*
BELOW: Un gran bell'arrosto, *1977, acrylic and oil on canvas, 61x91.5 cm (Private Collection)*

ABOVE: Still Life: Spring Fashion, *1978, acrylic on canvas, 61x76.2 cm (Private Collection);*
BELOW: Still Life: Autumn Fashion, *1978, acrylic on canvas, 61x76 cm (Walker Art Gallery)*

Unfinished Painting, *1978, acrylic on canvas, 76.2x91.4 cm (Private Collection)*

Town and Country, *1979, acrylic on canvas, 231.1x165.1 cm (Private Collection)*

Dining/Kitchen/Living, *1980, acrylic on canvas, 180x180 cm (Tochigi Prefectural Museum of Fine Arts)*

Selected Grapes, 1981, acrylic and oil on canvas, 38.4x60.6 cm (The British Council)

Candle-lit Dinner, *1981-82, acrylic on canvas, 76.2x61 cm (Private Collection)*

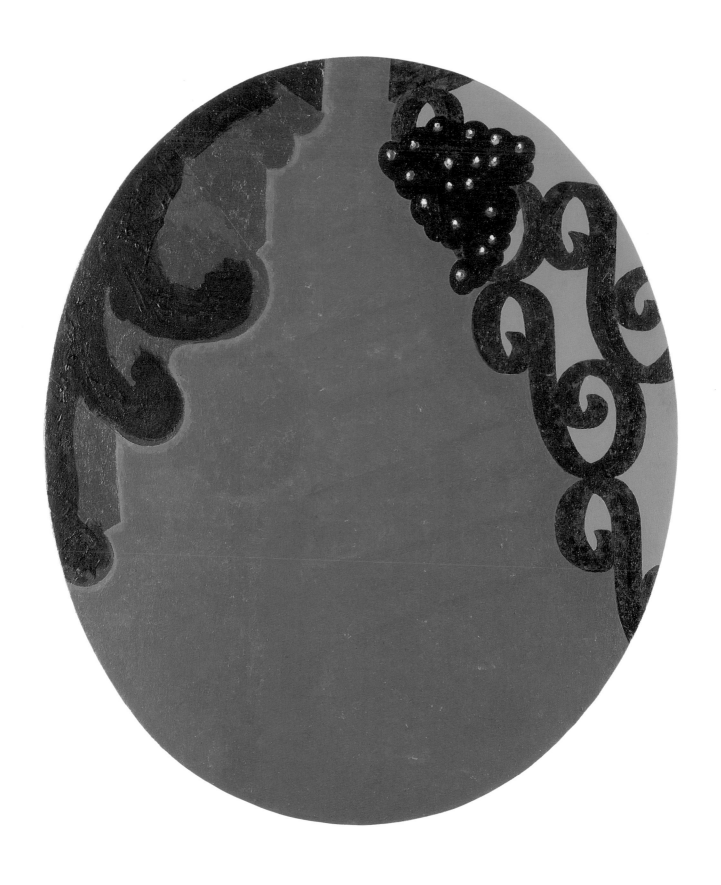

Smoky Interior, 1983, acrylic on canvas, 73.7x61 cm (Waddington Galleries)

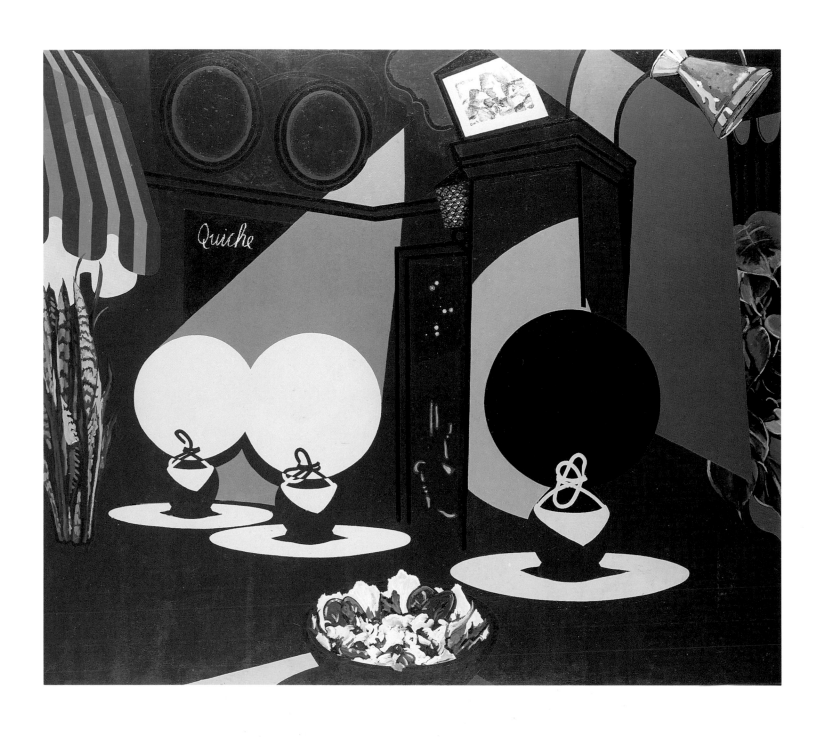

Wine Bar, *1983, acrylic on canvas, 182.9x213.4 cm (Private Collection)*

ABOVE: Green Drink, *1984, oil on canvas, 76.2x111.8 cm (Private Collection, London);*
BELOW: Eggs and Coffee, *1984, oil on canvas, 76.2x111.8 cm (Private Collection)*

FLOCK!!

ABOVE: Interior with a Picture, *1985-86, acrylic on canvas, 205.7x243.9 cm (Private Collection);*
BELOW: Lunch-time, *1985, acrylic on canvas, 205.7x243.8 cm (Saatchi Collection)*

Buffet, *1987, acrylic on canvas, 274.3x205.7 cm (Waddington Galleries)*

Glass of Whisky, *1987, acrylic on canvas, 76.2x111.7 cm (Saatchi Collection)*

Reception, *1988, acrylic on canvas, 304.8x205.8 cm (Waddington Galleries)*

Patio, *1988, acrylic on canvas, 73.6x61 cm (Howard Hodgkin, London)*

Grill, 1988, acrylic on canvas, 121.9x91.4 cm (Collection Janet de Botton, London)

Lantern, *1988, acrylic on canvas, 121.9x91.4 cm (Collection Elliot K Wolk, New York)*

The Blue Posts, *1989, acrylic on canvas, 289.5x205.7 cm (The British Council)*

Lounge, *1989, acrylic on canvas, 289.5x205.7 cm (Waddington Galleries)*

Lamp and Lung-Ch'uan Ware, *1989, acrylic on board, 77.5x52.1 cm (Waddington Galleries)*

Large White Jug, *1989, acrylic on board, 77.5x52.1 cm (Waddington Galleries)*

Pipe and Panel, *1990, acrylic on board, 35.2x28.8 cm (Private Collection)*

Pipe and Door, *1990, acrylic on canvas, 52x38 cm (Waddington Galleries)*

Pipe with Smoke, *1990, acrylic on board, 35.2x23.2 cm (The artist, courtesy of Waddington Galleries)*

Pipe and Diamond Shutter, *1990, acrylic on canvas, 76.2x61 cm (Waddington Galleries)*

Black Light with Letter, *1990, acrylic on canvas, 91.7x68.9 cm (The artist, courtesy of Waddington Galleries)*

Desk, *1991, acrylic on canvas, 274.3x213.4 cm (The artist, courtesy of Waddington Galleries)*

Claret, *1992, acrylic on canvas, 61x79.2 cm (The artist, courtesy of Waddington Galleries)*

ABOVE: Second Glass of Whisky, *1992, acrylic on canvas, 61x79.2 cm (Waddington Galleries);*
BELOW: Night Pipe, *1992, acrylic on canvas, 61x79.2 cm (Waddington Galleries)*

Study, *1992, acrylic on canvas, 61x79.2 cm (Private Collection)*

PATRICK CAULFIELD

Biographical Details

1936 Born in London 29 January
1956-60 Chelsea School of Art, London
1960-63 Royal College of Art, London
1963-71 Taught at Chelsea School of Art
1983 Commissioned to design the London Life mural, for The London Life Association's new headquarters in Bristol
1984 Commissioned to design the sets and costumes for Michael Corder's new ballet 'Party Games' at the Royal Opera House, Covent Garden
1986 Selected 'The Artist's Eye' at the National Gallery, London

Lives and works in London

One-Person Exhibitions

1965 Robert Fraser Gallery, London

1966 Robert Elkon Gallery, New York

1967 Robert Fraser Gallery, London
Studio Marconi, Milan

1968 Robert Elkon Gallery, New York

1969 Waddington Galleries, London (prints)

1971 Waddington Galleries, London
DM Gallery, London (prints)

1972 Sweeney Reed Galleries, Victoria, Australia

1973 Europalia, Brussels
Waddington Galleries, London (print retrospective)
DM Gallery, London (prints)

1974 OK Harris Works of Art, New York

1975 Waddington Galleries, London
Scottish Arts Council Gallery, Edinburgh
Bluecoat Gallery, Liverpool (prints)

1976 Arnolfini Gallery, Bristol

1977 Tortue Gallery, Santa Monica, California, touring to Phoenix Art Museum, Arizona (print retrospective)

1978 Tate Gallery, London (prints)

1979 Waddington Galleries, London

1980 IAC, Basle
Tolarno Galleries, Melbourne
Hughes Gallery, Brisbane; touring to Mona Gallery, Melbourne
Gardner Centre for the Arts, University of Sussex, Brighton; touring to Midland

Group, Nottingham; Oriel, Cardiff (Welsh Arts Council print exhibition)

1981 Walker Art Gallery, Liverpool; touring to Tate Gallery, London (retrospective)
Waddington Galleries, London (print retrospective)

1982 Nishimura Gallery, Tokyo (retrospective)

1983 Arnolfini Gallery, Bristol (print retrospective)

1985 Waddington Galleries, London

1985-87 National Museum of Fine Art, Rio de Janeiro (British Council print retrospective); touring to Federal University Espirito Santo, Vitoria, Brazil; University of Campinãs, Brazil; Museum of São Paulo; Palacio das Artes, Belos Horizonte, Brazil; Sociedade Brasileira Cultura Inglesa, Londrina; Cultural Foundation of Curitba, Brazil; Cultural Foundation of Santa Catarina, Florianopolis, Brazil; Institute of Arts of Federal University of Rio Grande do Sul, Porto Alegre, Brazil; Museo Naçional de Artes Plasticas y Visuales, Montevideo, Uraguay; Instituto Cultural de Las Condes, Santiago, Chile; Sala Vina, Vina del Mar, Chile; Museo de Bellas Artes, Concepçion, Chile

1988 Cleveland Gallery, Middlesborough (print retrospective)

1989 Waddington Galleries, London; touring to Tony Shafrazi Gallery, New York

1989-90 Fundaçao Calouste Gulbenkian, Lisbon (continuation of 1987 British Council print retrospective); touring to Guimares, North Portugal; Serrales Foundation, Oporto

1991-92 Kilburn Tricycle Gallery, London (prints)

1992 Serpentine Gallery, London

Group Exhibitions

1961 'Young Contemporaries', RBA Galleries, London

1962 'Young Contemporaries', RBA Galleries, London

1963 'Young Contemporaries', RBA Galleries, London

1964 'The New Generation', Whitechapel Art Gallery, London

1965 '4 Biennale, Salon de la Jeune Peinture', Musée d'Art Moderne, Paris (Prix des Jeunes Artistes for Graphics)
'Saison de la Nouvelle Peinture Anglaise – Patrick Caulfield/Derek Boshier', Galerie Aujourd'hui, Brussels

1966 'Robert Fraser Gallery at Studio Marconi', Studio Marconi, Milan
'Recent Still Life', Rhode Island School of Design, Museum of Art, New York

1967 'Jeunes Peintres Anglais', Palais des Beaux Arts, Brussels
'Drawing Towards Painting 2', Arts Council Gallery, London; touring to Stoke-on-Trent; Northampton; Oldham; Cardiff; St Ives; Reading; Liverpool; Bradford;

Norwich; Scarborough; Glasgow
'9 Bienal de Sao Paolo', São Paulo, Brazil
'5 Biennale des Jeunes Artistes', Musée d'Art Moderne, Paris
'1st Edinburgh Open 100 Exhibition', Edinburgh
'Recent British Painting', Peter Stuyvesant
Foundation Collection, Tate Gallery, London

1968 'Junge Generation Gross Britannien', Akademie der Kunste, Berlin
'The Obsessive Image', Institute of Contemporary Arts, London
'Painting 1964-67', Hayward Gallery, London
'X Mostra Internazionale di Bianco e Nero', Lugano
'Painted in Britain', ICA Exhibition, New York

1969 'Marks on a Canvas', Museum am Ostwall, Dortmund
'Pop Art', Hayward Gallery, London
'John Moores Liverpool Exhibition 7', Walker Art Gallery, Liverpool
'12 Britische Artisten', Kunstlerhaus Galerie, Vienna
'House Exhibition', Waddington Galleries, London

1971 'Junge Englander: Monro, Hoyland, Tucker,
Caulfield, Smith', Kunstudio Westfalen, Bielefeld, West Germany
'Patrick Caulfield, Ivon Hitchens, John Hoyland', Bear Lane Gallery, Oxford

1972 'Caulfield, Hodgkin, Moon', Galerie Stadler, Paris
'Fourteen BIG Prints', Bernard Jacobson Gallery, London

1973 'La Peinture Anglaise Aujourd'hui', Musée d'Art Moderne de la
Ville de Paris

1974 'British Painting '74', Hayward Gallery, London

1975 'Britianniasta 75', Taidehalli, Helsinki, Finland; touring to Alvar Aalto-
Museo, Jyvaskla; Taidemuseo, Tampere
'Body and Soul: Peter Moores Liverpool Project 3', Walker Art Gallery, Liverpool

1976 'Arte Inglese Oggi', Palazzo Reale, Milan
'Royal Academy Summer Show', Royal Academy of Arts, London

1977 'New Prints: Patrick Caulfield, Bernard Cohen,
Kenneth Martin, John Walker', Waddington and Tooth Graphics, London
'1977 Hayward Annual', Hayward Gallery, London

1978 'John Moores Liverpool Exhibition 11', Walker Art Gallery, Liverpool
'Groups', Waddington Galleries, London

1979 'Groups II', Waddington Galleries, London
'Understanding Prints', Waddington Galleries, London

1980 '1980 Hayward Annual', Hayward Gallery, London
'Groups III', Waddington Galleries, London
'Kelpra Studio: The Rose and Chris Prater Gift', Tate Gallery, London

1981 'Groups IV', Waddington Galleries, London

1982 'Aspects of British Art Today', Tokyo Metropolitan Art Museum, touring to
Tochigi Prefectural Museum of Fine Arts, Utsunomiya; National Museum of Art,
Osaka; Fukuoka Art Museum; Hokkaido Museum of Modern Art, Sapporo
'Groups V', Waddington Galleries, London

1983 'Groups VI', Waddington Galleries, London

1984 'Groups VII', Waddington Galleries, London
'British Artist's Books 1970-83', Atlantis Gallery, London
'The Proper Study', Lalit Kala Akademi, Delhi; touring to Jehangir Nicholson
Museum of Modern Art, Bombay
'Works on Paper', Waddington Galleries, London

1985 'Groups VIII', Waddington Galleries, London
'18 Bienal de Sao Paolo', Brazil, organised by the British Council, (with Stuart
Brisley, John Davies and Paula Rego)
'The Irresistible Object: Still Life 1600-1985', Leeds City Art Gallery

1986 'Forty Years of Modern Art 1945-1985', Tate Gallery, London
'The Artist's Eye', National Gallery, London
'Little and Large', Waddington Galleries, London

1987 'British Art in the Twentieth Century: The Modern Movement', Royal
Academy of Arts, London
'Pop Art USA – UK: American and British artists of the 60s in the 80s', Odakyu
Grand Gallery, Tokyo; Daimaru Museum, Osaka; Funabashi Seibu
Museum of Art, Funabashi; Sogo Museum of Art, Yokohama
'The Turner Prize', Tate Gallery, London
'2D/3D – Art and Craft Made and Designed for the Twentieth Century', Laing Art
Gallery, Newcastle and Northern Centre for Contemporary Art, Sunderland
'Black & White', Nicola Jacobs Gallery, London

1988 'Exhibition Road', 150th Anniversary Exhibition, Royal College
of Art, London
'Bridge', University of Lethbridge, Calgary
'Walia', Memorial Exhibition, Chelsea School of Art Gallery, London

1988-89 '100 Years of Art in Britain', Leeds City Art Gallery

1989 'Sun, Moon, Stars', Trelissick Gallery, Truro, Cornwall

1990 'Glasgow's Great British Art Exhibition', McLellan Galleries, Glasgow
'The 1990 Contemporary British Painters Exhibition', Business Design Centre,
Islington, London

1990-91 'For a Wider World: Sixty Works in the British Council Collection', The
British Council, Ukrainian National Museum, Kiev

1991 'British Art from 1930', Waddington Galleries, London
'The Absent Presence', Graves Art Gallery, Sheffield; touring to Geffrye
Museum, London
'Works for the Stage', Music Theatre Gallery, London
'Not Pop/What the Others Were Doing', Bernard Jacobson Gallery, London
'Five Artists', Waddington Galleries, London
'Contemporary Master Graphics', Lamont Gallery, London
'The 2nd Green Contemporary Art Sale', Smith's Galleries, London
'Art & Dance', Ferens Art Gallery, Hull

1991-92 'Pop Art', Royal Academy of Arts, London; touring to Museum Ludwig at
Kunsthalle Cologne and Centro de Arte Reina Sofia, Madrid

1992 'Ready, Steady, Go; Painting of the Sixties from the Arts Council Collec-
tion', Royal Festival Hall, London; and subsequent British tour
'Ten British Painters of the Twentieth Century', Music Theatre Gallery, London
Summer Exhibition, Royal Academy of Arts, London

Public Collections

Harry N Abrams Collection, New York; Arts Council of Great Britain, London;
Art Gallery of Western Australia, Perth; British Council, London; Calouste
Gulbenkian Foundation, Lisbon; Castle Museum, Norwich; Dallas Museum,
Texas; Delaware Art Museum, Delaware; Department of the Environment,
London; Hirshhorn Museum and Sculpture Garden, Smithsonian Institution,
Washington DC; Kunsthalle Bielefeld, West Germany; Manchester City Art
Gallery; National Gallery of Australia, Canberra; Scottish National Gallery of
Modern Art, Edinburgh; Peter Stuyvesant Foundation, London; Tate Gallery,
London; Victoria and Albert Museum, London; Virginia Museum of Fine Arts,
Richmond; Walker Art Gallery, Liverpool; Whitworth Art Gallery, Manchester

Bibliography

1964 Thompson, David: (introduction) *The New Generation*, catalogue, Whitechapel Gallery, London

1965 Burr, James: (review of exhibition at Robert Fraser Gallery) *Apollo*, January, p 55
Russell, John: (review of exhibition at Robert Fraser Gallery) *The Sunday Times*, 31 January
Russell, John: (review of exhibition at Robert Fraser Gallery) *ARTnews*, March, p 25
Rykwert, Joseph: (review of exhibition at Robert Fraser Gallery) *Domus*, March, p 55
Amaya, Mario: *Pop as Art*, Studio Vista, London, p 115

1966 Finch, Christopher: 'The Paintings of Patrick Caulfield' *Art International*, January, pp 47-49
Finch, Christopher: 'From Illusion to Allusion', *Art and Artists*, April, pp 20-22
'Patrick Caulfield', (review of Caulfield exhibition at Robert Elkon Gallery, New York) *Arts*, May, p 62
'Patrick Caulfield', (review of Caulfield exhibition at Robert Elkon Gallery, New York) *ARTnews*, May, p 15

1967 *Paintings by Patrick Caulfield*, catalogue, Robert Fraser Gallery, London
Finch, Christopher: 'Spotlight on Patrick Caulfield', *Vogue*, May, pp 112-114
Caulfield, Patrick: 'Why do artists make prints?', *Studio International* (supplement), June
'Patrick Caulfield', (review of Caulfield exhibition at Studio Marconi, Milan) *Domus*, August, p 39
Glazebrook, Mark: 'Pop-Kinky/Pop-Classical', *London Magazine*, September, pp 62-67
Lynton, Norbert: 'Caulfield Exhibition', *The Guardian*, 6 December
Brett, Guy: 'Caulfield's New Paintings', *The Times*, 7 December
Robertson, Bryan: 'Custom Built', *The Spectator*, 8 December

1968 Melville, Robert: (review of exhibition at Robert Fraser Gallery) *Architectural Review*, April, p 294
'Patrick Caulfield', (review of Caulfield exhibition at Robert Elkon Gallery, New York) *Arts*, June/Summer, p 64
'Patrick Caulfield', (review of Caulfield exhibition at Robert Elkon Gallery, New York) *ARTnews*, September, p 11

1969 Seymour, Anne: *Marks on a Canvas*, catalogue, Museum des 20. Jahrhunderts, Vienna
Lynton, Norbert: 'Patrick Caulfield exhibition', *The Guardian*, 10 January
Thomas, Robert: 'Graphics', *Art and Artists*, January, p 57
Kenedy, RC: 'London Letter', *Art International*, March, p 47
Brett, Guy: 'A painted window in Cork Street', *The Times*, 20 October
Lynton, Norbert: 'Caulfield', *The Guardian*, 22 October
Wright, Barbara: 'Patrick Caulfield/Waddington Gallery', *Arts Review*, 25 October
Denvir, Bernard: 'London Letter', *Art International*, December, p 69
Finch, Christopher: 'Patrick Caulfield', *Image as Language*, Penguin Books, Middlesex

1970 Thomas, R: 'Graphics: Chris Prater', *Art and Artists*, July, pp 46-47
Burr, James: (review of Caulfield at Waddington Galleries) *Apollo*, September, p 225
Tall, William: 'New Art From the Laboratory', *Detroit Free Press*, Detroit, 13 September

1971 Gosling, Nigel: 'Dandy with a Difference', *The Observer*, 19 December
Russell, John: 'Faces of England', *The Sunday Times*, 5 December
Ebeling, Rago T: 'Junge Englander: Monro, Hoyland, Tucker, Caulfield, Smith', catalogue, Kunstudio, Westfalen, Bielefeld, West Germany
Brett, Guy: 'How Professional', *The Times*, 14 December

Gilmour, Pat: 'Patrick Caulfield/DM Gallery and Waddington', *Arts Review*, 18 December
Finch, Christopher: *Patrick Caulfield*, Penguin New Art 2, Penguin Books, London

1972 Croydon, Blanche: 'Patrick Caulfield/Exe Gallery, Exeter', *Arts Review*, 15 January
Patrick Caulfield: Paintings and Prints, catalogue, Sweeney Reed Galleries, Victoria, Australia
Feaver, William: (review of Caulfield exhibition at Waddington Galleries) *Art International*, 20 February
Melville, Robert: 'The Religion of Art', *Architectural Review*, March, pp 87-88
Pluchart, François: 'Constantes et diversites britanniques', *Combat* (Paris), 27 March
Warnod, Jeanine: 'Les Arts: Mercredi, Rive Gauche', *Le Figaro*, 29 March
Breerette, Genevieve: 'Les Arts', *Le Monde*, 29 March
Reichardt, Jasia: 'Caulfield's pictorial theatre', *Architectural Design*, April, p 204
Wolfram, Eddie: 'Look and See', *Arts Review*, 8 April

1973 Laforgue, Jules: *The Poems of Jules Laforgue* (a book containing 12 poems by Jules Laforgue and 22 screenprints by Patrick Caulfield), Petersburg Press, London
Russell, John: 'Marriage of Equals', *The Sunday Times*, 29 April
Smart, Richard: 'Patrick Caulfield/Waddington', *Arts Review*, 5 May
'Caulfield's impressive production', (review of Caulfield exhibition at Waddington Galleries), *ARTnews*, Summer, p 86
Hobhouse, Janet: 'Patrick Caulfield "Print Retrospective" at the Waddington Gallery', *Studio International*, July/August, p 45
Cochrane, Candy: 'Patrick Caulfield/DM Gallery', *Arts Review*, 15 December
Reise, Barbara: 'Patrick Caulfield Prints', *Studio International*, December, p 227

1974 Packer, William: (review of Caulfield exhibition at DM Gallery) *Art and Artists*, January, pp 39-40
Cochrane, Candy: 'Patrick Caulfield/Atmosphere', *Arts Review*, 19 April
Loring, John: 'Comic Strip Pop', *Arts Magazine*, New York, September, pp 48-50
'Patrick Caulfield' (review of Caulfield exhibition at OK Harris, New York) *Arts*, December, p 12

1975 *Patrick Caulfield: Recent Paintings*, catalogue, Waddington Galleries, London
Lynton, Norbert: *Patrick Caulfield: Paintings and Prints*, catalogue, Scottish Arts Council Gallery, Edinburgh
Gilbert-Rolfe, Jeremy: (review of Caulfield exhibition at OK Harris, New York) *Artforum*, January, pp 73-74
Derfner, Phyllis: (review of Caulfield exhibition at OK Harris) *Art in America*, January/February, p 86, (extract reprinted in *Arte inglese oggi*, catalogue, Palazzo Reale, Milan, 1976)
Ingham, Margo: 'Patrick Caulfield/Bluecoat Gallery, Liverpool', *Arts Review*, 24 January
Feaver, William: 'Patrick Caulfield', *The Observer*, 30 November
Overy, Paul: 'What has Britain given to modern art?', *The Times*, 2 December
Vaizey, Marina: 'Discoveries' (review of Caulfield exhibition at Waddington Galleries), *The Sunday Times*, 7 December
Blakeston, Oswell: 'Caulfield', *Arts Review*, 12 December
McEwen, John: 'Live Style', *The Spectator*, 13 December
Packer, William: 'Patrick Caulfield', *The Financial Times*, 15 December (reprinted in *Arnolfini Magazine*, 17 February 1976)
Cork, Richard: 'What the geometry man and traditional Pat have in common', *Evening Standard*, 18 December
Melville, Robert: 'In our time' (review of Caulfield exhibition at Waddington Galleries) *New Statesman*, 19 December

1976 'Patrick Caulfield' (review of Caulfield exhibition at Waddington Galleries) *ARTnews*, February, p 101
Crichton, Fenella: 'Patrick Caulfield at Waddington Galleries', *Art International*, February/March, pp 45-46

Adams, Clive: 'Pop/Progressive', *Arnolfini Magazine* (Bristol), 17 February
Morris, Lynda: 'Hodgkin and Caulfield', *The Listener*, 1 April
Feaver, William: 'Artist's view', *Observer Magazine*, 8 August
Lynton, Norbert: 'Patrick Caulfield', *Arte Inglese Oggi 1960-76*, catalogue, Palazzo Reale, Milan

1977 Oliver, G: 'Et après Bacon?', *Connaissance des Arts*, June, pp 96-103
Whittet, GS: 'Patrick Caulfield', *Contemporary Artists*, St James Press, London
Patrick Caulfield Print Retrospective: Complete Works 1964-1976, catalogue, Tortue Gallery, Santa Monica
Shone, Richard: *The Century of Change: British Painting since 1900*, Phaidon Press, Oxford

1978 Simmons, Rosemary: 'Patrick Caulfield Prints/Tate Gallery, London', *Arts Review*, 27 October, p 578

1979 *Patrick Caulfield, Recent Paintings*, catalogue, Waddington Galleries, London
Packer, William: 'Patrick Caulfield and Others', *Financial Times*, 3 July
Feaver, William: 'The Seal of Approval', *The Observer*, 15 July
Burr, James: 'A Talent in English Painting', *Apollo*, July, p 74
Blakeston, Oswell: 'Patrick Caulfield/Waddington II', *Arts Review*, 20 July
Shepherd, Michael: 'Out of the ordinary', *What's on in London*, 20 July
Kent, Sarah: 'Caulfield/Waddington', *Time Out*, 20-26 July
McEwen, John: 'Caulfield', *The Spectator*, 21 July
Shepherd, Michael: 'Some Common Touches', *The Sunday Telegraph*, 22 July
Crichton, Fenella: 'London: Patrick Caulfield/Waddington', *Art and Artists*, September, p 38
Quantrill, Malcolm: 'London: Spring-Summer', *Art International*, September, p 73
Caulfield, Patrick: 'Painting today: a questionnaire', *London Magazine*, April/May
Gilmour, Pat: 'Screenprint', *Understanding Prints: A Contemporary Guide*, Waddington Galleries, London

1980 Hyman, Timothy: 'Caulfield's Laforgue', *Artscribe*, August, pp 16-20
'Hangovers and gunfighters', *Australian*, 19 February
Patrick Caulfield: The Complete Graphics 1964-80, catalogue, Oriel, Cardiff
Massie, Rebecca: *The Lewis Contemporary Art Fund Collection*, Virginia Museum of Fine Arts, Richmond

1981 Robertson, Bryan: (introduction) *Patrick Caulfield: Prints 1964-81*, catalogue, Waddington Galleries, London
Livingstone, Marco: (interview with Patrick Caulfield) *Aspects*, no 15, Summer
Feaver, William: 'Rich entertainments', *Observer Magazine*, 25 October
Packer, William: 'Scotland the Brave', *Financial Times*, 3 November
Berthoud, Roger: 'Where next for Caulfield?', *The Times*, 4 November
McEwen, John: 'Man of Irony', *Spectator*, 7 November
Shepherd, Michael: 'Wry Whiskey', *What's on in London*, 11 December
Russell Taylor, John: (review of 'Prints 1964-81' at Waddington Graphics), *The Times*, 17 November
Shepherd, Michael: 'Two at the Tate', *The Sunday Telegraph*, 15 November
McEwen, John: (review of Tate Gallery retrospective exhibition) *Art Monthly*, December/January 1982
'The Shock of the Familiar', *Over 21*, November
Baker, Steve: 'Patrick Caulfield at the Walker Art Gallery, Liverpool', *Artscribe*, no 31
Bumpus, Judith: 'Patrick Caulfield talks to Judith Bumpus', *The Connoisseur*, October

1981-82 Livingstone, Marco: 'Patrick Caulfield', *Patrick Caulfield, Paintings 1963-81*, catalogue, Tate Gallery, London, and Walker Art Gallery, Liverpool

1982 Rose, Andrea: 'Air on a G-Plan: Patrick Caulfield at Mid-Term', *The London Magazine*, volume 21, no 11, February
Okada, Takahiko: *Patrick Caulfield, 1969-1981*, catalogue, Nishimura Gallery, Tokyo

1983 Biggs, Lewis: 'Patrick Caulfield: Prints', *Anolfini Magazine*, March

1984 Burr, James: 'Round the Galleries: The Most Revealing Things We Do', *Apollo*, April
'Party Game', *About the House* (Magazine of the Friends of Covent Garden), Christmas, pp 46-47

1985 Burr, James: 'Round the Galleries: Paint for Paint's Sake', *Apollo*, January
Feaver, William: 'Soft touches, hard covers', *The Observer*, 14 April
Vaizey, Marina: 'The dishes of the day', *The Sunday Times*, 7 April
Kent, Sarah: (review of Caulfield show at Waddington Galleries, London), *Time Out*, 11 April
Packer, William: 'Win or Lose, it's the best', *The Financial Times*, 23 April
McEwen, John: 'Patrick Caulfield', *18 Bienal de Sao Paulo*, Sao Paulo, catalogue (organised by the British Council)
Hicks, Alistair: 'Patrick Caulfield', *Mercury*, March/April
Burr, James: 'Round the Galleries: The Ugly Face of Power', *Apollo*, April
Spurling, John: 'Adults only', *New Statesman*, 19 May
Kent, Sarah: 'Waddington – Patrick Caulfield', *Time Out*, 18 April
Patrick Caulfield, catalogue, Waddington Galleries, London
Russell Taylor, John: 'Lack of inhibition fit to make the earth tremble', *The Times*, 16 April

1986 Checkland, Sarah Jane: 'An artist with a quixotic eye', *The Times*, 31 May
Mitchelmore, Ros: 'Patrick Caulfield: A touch of realism', *The Artist's and Illustrator's Magazine*, no 1, October
MDA: 'Un artista con un lenguaje sin tiempo', *La Manana*, 7 September
De Espada, Roberto: 'Mundo refinado y poetico de Caulfield', *El Dia*, 4 September
'Mas de 60,000 Personas en Muestra del Ermitage que Exhibe el Museo Nacional', *El Pais*, 6 September
Haber, Alicia: 'Cantan Los Objetos', *El Pais*, 7 September
'Caulfield y Grandes del Renacimiento', *El Diario*, 12 September
Haber, Alicia: 'Naturalezas No Tan Muertas', *El Pais*, 14 September
Roubaud, Elisa: 'Color, Humor, Virtuosismo', *El Pais*, 9 September
Peluffo, Gabriel: 'El discreto encanto de la serigrafia', *Brecha*, 12 September

1988 Morris, Ann: 'The Experts' Expert: The discerning palette', *Observer Magazine*, 15 May

1989 Robertson, Bryan: 'Introducao' (introduction), *Patrick Caulfield: Serigrafias*, catalogue, Fundacao Calouste Gulbenkian, Lisbon
Fallon, Brian: 'Painter of the pop age', *Irish Times*, 18 October
Hicks, Alistair: *New British Art in the Saatchi Collection*, Thames & Hudson, London
Feaver, William: 'Blue local with no pub furniture', *The Observer*, 17 September
Burr, James: 'Around The Galleries', *Apollo*, September, pp 207-208
Lucie-Smith, Edward: 'Warhol's hidden parts revealed', *The Independent*, 18 September
Wakely, Shelagh: 'Patrick Caulfield, Waddingtons', *Time Out*, 13-20 September
Russell, John: 'Patrick Caulfield', *New York Times*, 13 October
Feaver, William: 'London: Patrick Caulfield', *ARTnews*, December, p 175

1990 Burn, Emma: 'Patrick Caulfield at the Music Theatre Gallery', *Arts Review*, 4 May, p 230

1991 Morgan, Stuart: 'Europop (Le Pop Art n'est pas ne au pays de l'Oncle Sam)', *Beaux Arts*, September, No 93, pp 76-
Livingstone, Marco: *Pop Art*, Royal Academy of Arts exhibition catalogue
'Patrick puts the pop in painting', *Pinner & Stanmore Observer*, 19 December

1992 'Ready, Steady, Go: Painting of the Sixties from the Arts Council Collection', Royal Festival Hall, Arts Council and South Bank Centre publication
'British Pop Art as Amusement Machine', *Bijutsu Techno* (Japan), Vol 44 No 651, March, p 48
Berryman, Larry: 'Ready, Steady, Go review', *Arts Review*, April, Vol XLIV, pp 112-113